PIONEER PROPHETESS

Jemima Wilkinson, the Publick Universal Friend

Jemima Wilkinson in 1816, painted by John L. D. Mathies. This portrait hangs in the Oliver House, Penn Yan, New York, in the collection of the Yates County Historical Society. Reproduced by courtesy of the Village Board, Penn Yan, N.Y.; not to be copied.

First published 1964

Library of Congress Catalog Card Number: 64-7875

PRINTED IN THE UNITED STATES OF AMERICA
BY KINGSPORT PRESS, INC.

Pioneer Prophet

Jemima Wilkinson,

the Publick Universal Fri

By HERBERT A. WISBEY,

Cornell University Pres

Ithaca, New York

FOR MY MOTHER
MARTHA MARIETTA BURGESS WISBEY

Preface

JEMIMA WILKINSON was one of three notable religious innovators who appeared in New England in the opening years of the American Revolution. The other two —John Murray, founder of Universalism in America, and Mother Ann Lee of the Shakers—left more enduring marks in American religious history, but Jemima Wilkinson, the only native American of the trio, also merits serious attention. This self-educated, penniless woman, who called herself the Publick Universal Friend, became a successful, nondenominational, evangelical preacher. Supported by people of wealth and social position whom she induced to follow her, she was the first American-born woman to found a religious society. Leading her group into the wilderness of western New York, she pioneered in settling that region as well as in attempting to establish a religious community apart from the secular world. Born just after the middle of the eighteenth century and living almost through the second decade of the nineteenth, Jemima Wilkinson deserves to be ranked with the small group of outstanding women of the colonial period.

For decades after her death her adherents and their

descendants followed her example of refusing to answer detractors. Nothing was written on her behalf, and the letters and journals of the Publick Universal Friend and those close to her were carefully hidden away. The only book devoted exclusively to Jemima Wilkinson was a small biography first published in 1821, and reprinted in 1844, which unfortunately contains some completely fictitious episodes and is largely inaccurate as to fact and misleading in interpretation.

Within the last few years some of the manuscript material relating to the Publick Universal Friend and her society became available. The present study is based on that material and on a careful survey of other sources—manuscript collections, diaries, town records, contemporary newspapers, and other printed matter. The sizable body of folklore about Jemima Wilkinson also was sifted in an attempt to separate fact from fiction. When the stories, oral as well as written, were analyzed, it became clear that this woman had acquired a folk characterization in addition to her historical personality, and that the folk image was quite different from the real person. To keep the two distinct, a chapter of this book is devoted to the lore and legends about Jemima Wilkinson.

This author, like Jemima Wilkinson, grew up in Rhode Island and, until recently, lived in the Jerusalem Township she founded. Over the last eight years he listened to stories about her, collected information about her life, and visited the various localities with which she was associated. A year of sabbatical leave from Keuka College was devoted to research on this book. Completion of the work was made possible by a grant-in-aid from the Research Council of the College Center of the Finger Lakes.

It would be impossible for the author to thank by name all the individuals who have assisted him. A list would include a host of librarians in public and college libraries, curators and staff members of historical societies, town and county clerks, and many individuals who owned papers or lived in houses or remembered stories associated with Jemima Wilkinson. Some of these are mentioned in the bibliographical notes; all deserve sincere thanks for their interest and friendly assistance. Special gratitude for the use of facilities and the exceptional helpfulness of the staffs is due to the John Hay Library of Brown University, the Rhode Island Historical Society, the Collection of Regional History of Cornell University, and the Keuka College Library. Special recognition also should be given to Mrs. Walter D. Henricks, of Penn Yan, who shared her wealth of information and experience and gave constant encouragement.

The Death Book of the society of Universal Friends is printed here for the first time, through the courtesy of its owner, Jay D. Barnes, of Penn Yan. The photograph of the portrait of Jemima Wilkinson which appears as the frontispiece is reproduced for the first time, with special permission from the Penn Yan Village Board of Trustees through arrangements made by Frank L. Swann, President of the Yates County Historical Society. My wife, Adelia W. Wisbey, who typed, edited, and criticized the manuscript in all stages of its development, deserves to be considered a collaborator in this book.

HERBERT A. WISBEY, JR.

Corning, New York
May 1964

Contents

Illustrations

DRAWINGS

PIONEER PROPHETESS

Jemima Wilkinson, the Publick Universal Friend

Chapter I

Birth of a Prophetess

THE story of Jemima Wilkinson's death and resurrection spread quickly from her native town of Cumberland throughout Rhode Island and the rest of New England. Tales of miraculous events have fascinated New Englanders since the days of Cotton Mather, and in that fall of 1776, as the familiar pattern of life was being destroyed by the beginnings of the American Revolution, this strange story was passed from person to person by word of mouth, with embellishments added in the process. Wherever she went in her distinctive costume, crowds packed the meetings held by this attractive young woman, whose call to preach, she maintained, had brought her back from the dead.

This eighteenth-century female Lazarus was deeply rooted in her native New England. Jemima Wilkinson belonged to the fourth generation of her family in America and was related by blood or marriage to many of the leading families in Rhode Island. Lawrence Wilkinson, the first of the family to settle in the colonies, came to Rhode Island about 1650; he was one of the early freemen and was active in the colonial government. Jemima's father, Jeremiah Wilkinson, was the youngest of six children of John Wilkinson and a first cousin to Stephen Hopkins, several times governor of the colony and signer of the Declaration of Independence, and to Esek Hopkins, first commander in chief of the American navy.

Jeremiah Wilkinson was born in 1707 at Martin's Wading Place, a ford across the Blackstone River, in the town of Smithfield, Rhode Island. He inherited land just east of the river in a section known as the Attleboro Gore, and between 1725 and 1739 cleared the title to his inheritance and bought adjoining property to make a sizable estate. The property, originally part of the Rehoboth North Purchase, was considered to be in the town of Attleboro, Massachusetts, although the whole section, which was known as the Gore, was in continual dispute between the colonies of Massachusetts and Rhode Island. Finally the disputed territory was awarded to Rhode Island by a royal commission, and in 1747 this part of it was incorporated as the town of Cumberland. Jeremiah Wilkinson's land and homestead in Cumberland was about a mile east of the Blackstone River, south of Hunting Hill and north of Camp Swamp, on a rise known as Cherry Hill. Jeremiah became well-to-do as a farmer and orchardist. The cherry trees he planted gave the hill its name and led to his being nicknamed "Cherry Wilkinson."

Amey Whipple Wilkinson, Jemima's mother, is a woman of mystery. The dates of her birth, marriage, and death were not recorded, and even her given name has been a subject of disagreement. Moses Brown, who knew the family and also collected material from Jemima's brother, Jeremiah, gave her name as Amey, the daughter of William Whipple. Her name was also listed as Amey when the birth dates of her children were recorded by the town clerk of Cumberland. Jeremiah and Amey Wilkinson probably were married about 1738, since the first of their children was born in 1739. It is doubtful that Amey Wilkinson was a member of the Society of Friends; no mention of any Whipple was found in a careful search of the records of the Smithfield monthly meeting, to which her husband belonged. According to Quaker custom, he should have appeared before the monthly meeting to declare his intention of marrying "according to the good order of Friends," but no such appearance or marriage is recorded. In describing Jemima Wilkinson's association with the Society of Friends, Moses Brown wrote: "The Father being a Member, Jemima was born such." Brown's failure to mention both parents strengthens the suspicion that her mother was not a Quaker.[1]

Amey Wilkinson spent her married life in almost continual childbearing, giving birth to twelve children in twenty-five years. The eighth child, her fourth daughter, was born on November 29, 1752, and was given the biblical name Jemima, after one of the daughters of Job.

Jemima was only twelve or thirteen when her mother died. Her youngest sister was born in August, 1764, and tradition has it that Amey Wilkinson died soon afterward. The death of the mother, worn out by childbearing, must have been a shock to the young girl and may have influenced Jemima's attitude toward sex and marriage later in her own life.

Little dependable information is available about Jemima Wilkinson's early years. The usual account, based on Hudson's unreliable biography, represents her as a great beauty, with a passion for fine clothes and gay company. She was supposed to be headstrong, excessively lazy, and ingenious in shifting her share of the household work to her sisters. Unfortunately, no contemporary evidence exists either to affirm or to contradict this portrayal. Its authenticity is questionable, however, as is the episode told about an unsuccessful career of about ten months as an apprentice tailoress.

Some conjectures about Jemima's girlhood may be deduced from her later life. Since she was an accomplished horsewoman, she undoubtedly began riding as a girl. Her strong, athletic figure must have been developed by working in the house and on the farm as well as walking and riding to town and to meeting. In later years, as a pioneer on the New York State frontier, she was able to pull one end of a crosscut saw to help cut logs into firewood. She also hoed and weeded her garden, picked berries, pulled grass for weaving baskets, and demonstrated other skills that reflected the experience of an active childhood on a New England farm. A farm child grows up close to nature. Near the Wilkinson home were rock ledges begging to be climbed for a view of orchards and fields held apart by stone walls; in the woods and swamp not far from the house grew ferns, Solomon's-seal, jack-in-the-pulpit, pungent skunk cabbage, and various herbs and berries that were used both as food and as medicine. Jemima Wilkinson must have begun as a girl to absorb medical lore and knowledge of folk cures, for in later life she was skilled in bringing relief from sickness and injury.

The most outstanding quality about young Jemima was her extraordinary memory. Although she had little formal education, she was an avid reader, especially of the Bible and of the classic works of Quaker theology and history. She studied her Bible so thoroughly that she could quote long sections of it almost verbatim; scriptural phrases became an integral part of her ordinary speech. Robert Barclay's *Apology* and the works of George Fox and William Penn were her textbooks. Undoubtedly she was thoroughly familiar also with William Sewel's history of the Quakers and Joseph Besse's account of their early persecutions and sufferings.

Jemima Wilkinson's Quaker heritage was unquestionably the strongest influence in her life. As a birthright member of the Society of Friends, she grew up in the faith that God could make His will known directly through the inner light in each individual. The books she read were full of testimonies of people to whom God had spoken in clear and unmistakable commands. "I have had," said George Fox, "a word from the Lord as the prophets and apostles had." The Quaker martyr Marmaduke Stephenson, who was hanged in Boston in 1659, wrote: "The Word of the Lord came to me in a still small Voice, which I did hear perfectly, saying to me,

in the Secret of my Heart and Conscience, *I have ordained thee a Prophet unto the Nation.*" This call came
when he was plowing. Women, too, received divine
commissions. Margaret Brewster, in 1677, was "raised up
as one from the dead, and came from a sick bed . . .
to bear a testimony and be as a sign to warn the bloody
town of Boston to end its cruel laws." Some of these
very phrases appeared in Jemima Wilkinson's own testimony later, as she explained her vision and her mission.

The Quaker heroes and heroines about whom Jemima
Wilkinson read lived a century or more before her day.
By the late eighteenth century, members of the Society
of Friends were more concerned with preserving themselves as a "peculiar people" than in proselyting. The
missionary zeal that caused the Massachusetts Puritans
so much discomfort and led to the martyrdom of both
men and women in Boston gave way to concern with
enforcing conformity to Quaker practice and preventing
the loss of members by marriage "outside the good order
of Friends." The family of Jemima Wilkinson belonged
to the Smithfield Lower Meeting, so called to distinguish
it from another Quaker meeting in the upper part of
the town. The meetinghouse where they worshiped was
about four miles from the Wilkinson home.[2] Membership
in the Society of Friends and attendance at the regular
weekly meetings for worship failed to provide Jemima
Wilkinson with a meaningful religious experience or to
bring her peace of mind, however.

When she was nearly eighteen, George Whitefield
passed through Rhode Island and Massachusetts on his
last tour of New England. She could have heard him
speak in either Providence or nearby Attleboro, and tra-

dition suggests that his preaching moved her to a positive religious experience. Unfortunately, there is no evidence to show that she had any actual contact with this stirring preacher, who sparked the Great Awakening in the colonies. It is not inaccurate to say that she came under his influence, however. The Great Awakening that began in the 1740's had much less effect in Rhode Island than in the other colonies of New England, but even here congregations were split and new churches were formed because of theological disputes. Groups of New Lights, also known as New Light Baptists or Separates, formed noisy, zealous congregations of persons emphasizing individual inspiration and enlightenment through the Holy Spirit. Hostile to all authority other than the Bible and the Holy Spirit, they were strict in requiring their members to give clear evidence of a conversion experience. New Light sermons were exhortations rather than expositions and were characterized by emotionalism, the preachers using whatever devices of voice or gesture they could to make their points.

Jemima Wilkinson joined such a group of New Lights in Cumberland, and her association with them as well as her Quaker heritage evidently shaped her own religious teachings. One result of her union with the New Lights was her expulsion from the Society of Friends. Jemima was taken under dealing in February, 1776, for not attending Friends' meetings and not using the plain language (*thee* and *thou*). As in every case of such discipline, a committee called on her and urged her to mend her ways. A letter of contrition and a return to Quaker practice certainly would have saved her membership, but Jemima, evidently, not only had stopped attending Quaker meetings and using the plain language but had no desire to change her course of action. She was disowned by the Smithfield monthly meeting in August, 1776, two months before her illness and vision. Her sister Patience was disowned at the same time for having an illegitimate child. The Quaker teachings of Jemima Wilkinson's childhood and her later experience with the New Lights conditioned her to accept the premise that God communicated His commands directly to the human spirit. Tradition suggests that she was in a state of spiritual unrest in the fall of 1776: she cut herself off from social contacts and spent her time studying the Bible and meditating.

The excitement of the times did not leave the Wilkinson household untouched. An elder brother, Benjamin Wilkinson, was promoted from ensign to lieutenant in the Cumberland company of militia, and was also a member of the local Committee of Safety. The youngest boys, Stephen and Jeptha, were brought under dealing by the Society of Friends in March, 1776, and dismissed in May, when it was shown that they "frequented Trainings for millitary Service and Endeavor to Justify the Same." Jeptha, it seems, had joined the minutemen in the defense of Boston the year before.

The British evacuated Boston in March, 1776, and for a time New England was free from British troops, although Captain James Wallace on the British warship "Rose" plundered the islands and coastline of Narragansett Bay and upset Rhode Island's regular commerce. Rhode Island declared its independence in May, 1776, anticipating the declaration of the Continental Congress by two months, and spent most of 1776 making futile plans for the defense of Newport, which the British occupied without a fight

in December. In these disturbing, uncertain, exciting
times, which involved members of her family as well as
neighbors and friends, Jemima could hardly have avoided
the family discussions on the merits of the colonial cause
as opposed to the British, the morality of bearing arms,
the question of independence and its consequences, and
even, perhaps, cousin Stephen Hopkins's role in the Continental Congress.

The atmosphere in the motherless Wilkinson household
could not have been helpful to this young woman of
twenty-three, deeply concerned about her spiritual condition. Patience Wilkinson's indiscretion must have disturbed the family and contributed to the tension, as the
boys prepared to fight the British in defiance of Quaker
principles. All year committees of Friends, sent by the
monthly meeting, visited the house to discuss the delin-
quencies of one or another of the members of the family.
Jemima Wilkinson, unsatisfied by association with the New
Lights and officially cut off from the fellowship of the
Society of Friends, was under great emotional stress. It is
not surprising that she became ill.

Accounts of her illness take several forms. One story
is that an epidemic struck the neighborhood and that she
threw all her energies into nursing the sick, predicting
that if she became sick herself she knew she would die.
Another is that she withdrew from all company more
and more, complaining of ill health and finally taking to
her bed although she showed no symptoms of physical
illness. The implications are that she either suffered from
a mental breakdown or was feigning illness in prepa-
ration for the announcement of her mission. David
Hudson, in his bitterly hostile and unreliable biography,

makes it clear that he believed her entire illness was feigned and her hallucinations self-induced. Many of the details that he gives, however, describe recognizable symptoms of mental illness. Her sickness was so serious that her family summoned Dr. Man from Attleboro, about six miles away. He later confirmed that she did have a fever and suggested that her mind had been affected. Moses Brown, who secured the doctor's account, wrote of it as follows:

Her Case was Like one other he knew of that the fever being Translated to the head She Rose with different Ideas that what She had when the fever was General, and she Conceived the Idea that she had been Dead and was raised Up for Extraordinary Purposes, and got well fast,—but, that She had been Dead none of her friends or Attendants had any apprehension or thought of her having been Dead, but She was for some time After Considered by her friends not to be in her right Mind.

Dr. Man's description of the case he treated discredits the stories that, at the height of her illness, Jemima Wilkinson lay in a deathlike state for several hours, or even days. Another ridiculous story, without any validity, is that she was actually placed in a coffin as dead and arose, dramatically, as she was about to be buried. The doctor's testimony that none of her family or attendants ever thought she was dead was confirmed by her older brother Jeremiah, in information he gave to Moses Brown. Not only was she believed not to be dead, but she was not even in a trance, he declared. Her sickness was a fever, he recalled, and she got well fast, and "immediately" began to preach and to collect followers.

It is clear from these accounts of her illness by people

who were actually present that the various stories of her "death," describing cataleptic or comatose periods of unconsciousness, ranging in length from as little as half an hour to as long as three days—the latter an obvious comparison to Christ—are fabrications. They are folk tales that many repeated and a few believed even while Jemima Wilkinson was alive. Her own account of her "fatal fever" shows that she herself believed that she had actually died and that the visions she experienced in the delirium of the fever were genuine revelations of the will of God. The following description of Jemima Wilkinson's illness and vision was found tucked into her Bible and was preserved with her papers:

A Memorandum of the introduction of that fatal Fever, call'd in the Year 1776, the Columbus fever: since call'd the Typus, or malignant fever:—The Ship call'd Columbus, which sail'd out of Providence, in the State of Rhode Island Being a Ship of war, on her return brought with her Prisoners. This Awful, and allarming disease, Of which many of the inhabitants in providence died: And has Since spread more universally across the Country. And on the fourth of the 10th. Month, it reached the house of Jemima Wilkison, ten Miles from Providence, In which this truly interesting and great event took place!

On the fourth Day of the 10th. Month, on the Seventh Day of the weak, at night, a certain young-woman, known by the name of Jemima Wilkison was seiz'd with this mortal disease. And on the 2d. Day of her illness, was render'd almost incapable of helping herself.—And the fever continuing to increase untill fifth Day of the Weak about midnight, She appear'd to meet the Shock of Death; which [illegible] the Soul.

This part of the account suggests that the "fatal Fever" was typhus. This may be true, but, while there were numerous newspaper references to outbreaks of smallpox and dysentery in Rhode Island in 1775 and 1776, no other mention than this may be found of either typhus or "Columbus fever." On the other hand, the ship "Columbus" was part of the Continental naval fleet and was in and out of its home port of Providence several times in 1776. It was commanded by Captain Abraham Whipple, possibly a kinsman of Jemima's, whose exploits were well known in Rhode Island. This memorandum also establishes the date of the illness. October 4, 1776, was a Friday, but if the illness began at night it might be said it began on the seventh day, or Saturday. The climax, according to the account, came on Thursday, October 10.

The vision that coincided with the height of the fever is described in great detail in the obscure, allegorical language typical of Jemima:

The heavens were open'd And She saw too Archangels decending from the east, with golden crowns upon there heads, clothed in long white Robes, down to the feet; Bringing a sealed Pardon from the living God; and putting their trumpets to their mouth, proclaimed saying, Room, Room, Room, in the many Mansions of eternal glory for Thee and for everyone, that there is one more call for, that the eleventh hour is not yet past with them, and the day of grace is not yet over with them. For every one that will come, may come, and partake of the waters of life freely, which is offered to Sinners without money, and without price.

An interesting confirmation of this part of the memorandum comes from her brother, who more than forty years later remembered her saying at the time of her illness, "There is Room Enough." It is likely that this memorandum represents the account that Jemima Wilkinson told to her devoted followers. Although Christ is not once mentioned by name, the implication is clear that her mission was to fill His role in her day.

And the Angels said, The time is at hand, when God will lift up his hand, a second time, to recover the remnant of his People, whos day is not yet over; and the Angels said, The Spirit of Life from God, had descended to earth, to warn a lost and guilty, perishing dying World, to flee from the wrath which is to come; and to give an Invitation to the lost Sheep of the house of Israel to come home; and was waiting to assume the Body which God had prepared, for the Spirit to dwell in. . . . And then taking her leave of the family between the hour of nine & ten in the morning dropt the dying flesh & yielded up the Ghost. And according to the declaration of the Angels,—the Spirit took full posession of the Body it now animates.

From this it seems certain that Jemima's concept of her experience involved more than a spiritual rebirth, or religious conversion, in the usual sense of the term. It was, she maintained, an actual physical death of the body and a resurrection similar to that of Lazarus, except that the body of Jemima Wilkinson now housed a new spirit, sent from God with a special mission. The Angels said, in the vision, "The time is at hand, when God will lift up his hand, *a second time* [italics added], to recover the remnant of his People, whos day is not yet over." If this was how she described her call to preach, it is not surprising that her message was interpreted to mean that, since Christ was the *first* sent by God to save the world, and that, since Jemima Wilkinson as the Universal Friend professed to be the *second*, she claimed to be Christ come again.

This illness, characterized by the vision which began

her new life and ministry, is the key to understanding her remarkable career as the Publick Universal Friend. All the trustworthy, available, contemporary evidence, as well as the testimony of the rest of her life, indicates that her illness was genuine. The fever from which she suffered may not have been typhus, but was certainly serious enough to require the attention of a doctor and neighbors to sit with her through the nights of her illness. Coming as it did after a long period of spiritual struggle and emotional turmoil, the fever was part of, or brought on, a mental disturbance that left the young woman under the influence of a form of megalomania until she finally "left time" forty-three years later. The delirious hallucinations of her feverish, troubled mind were, to her, a vision from God, so real that she was able to record it in detail after she recovered. She was under its influence when, after the fever left her, she announced to her startled attendants that the old Jemima Wilkinson was dead and that a new spirit inhabited her body. This reborn spirit was to be called the Publick Universal Friend, whose mission it was to preach to a sinful and dying world. She called for her clothes and dressed, and except for this curious religious monomania soon appeared to be well again.

On the Sunday after her vision (October 13, 1776, according to her memorandum) Jemima Wilkinson, now the Universal Friend, attended meeting at the Elder Miller Meeting House at Abbott Run, about three miles from her home. This little Baptist meetinghouse was the second oldest church edifice in Cumberland and may have housed the New Light congregation with which Jemima was associated. Undoubtedly she was a center of curious attention from those who knew of her illness and had heard of her supposed death. After the service she addressed a group of the congregation under a large shade tree in the churchyard, her first public sermon. There was nothing heretical or even startling about what she said, although her confidence and poise were surprising. She spoke with great assurance and conviction about what constituted a moral life, the dangers of sin, and the need for repentance. The ministry of the Publick Universal Friend was launched.

In the weeks that followed this initial appearance, Jemima Wilkinson held meetings in her own home and traveled to nearby towns, speaking in private houses and in public places. Although as the Universal Friend she no longer recognized her father or any of her brothers or sisters as having a special relationship to her, her father accompanied her on these excursions, probably out of concern for her safety. Such "going about" with his daughter brought him a warning from the Society of Friends, which, having expelled Jemima before her vision, now considered her preaching a dangerous heresy. When Jeremiah Wilkinson failed to make satisfactory explanation to the committee who called upon him, he too was disowned, in September, 1777.[3] Jemima Wilkinson's first real converts were members of her own family. Eventually four of her sisters and a brother, Stephen, joined her and followed her throughout her ministry. These four sisters were unmarried in 1776. Deborah, the youngest, was only twelve and Elizabeth was sixteen, but Marcy (or Mercy) was twenty-six and Patience was an impatient twenty-nine. Patience had been disowned by the Society of Friends earlier, and now Marcy, Elizabeth, and Deborah were considered for discipline. All three girls were visited and reasoned with but indicated that they preferred Jemima's meetings to those of the Quakers. Marcy, in particular, demonstrated an unbecoming flippancy in talking with the committee sent to "labour" with her. She did not know if she should attend any more of their meetings, she told them, and she had not planned to come the last time, "but as it was on the way fell in." If she was a bother to Friends, she had nothing against their disowning her as a member of the society, she declared. All three girls were dismissed between 1778 and 1779. It is hard to see what benefits the sisters and brother could have anticipated by following the religious teachings of Jemima, who at this time had not a penny of her own and was regarded as sadly demented by many of the local people.

For about two years after her vision, Jemima Wilkinson lived at home in Cumberland and there received visitors and planned her trips. She prayed loudly in the dead of night, reported Moses Brown, who heard her while visiting her father in the summer of 1777. Most of her travels in this period were in the region east of Narragansett Bay in Rhode Island and nearby Massachusetts. Ezra Stiles heard of her in 1776, when he lived in Dighton, Massachusetts, and heard that she preached in Swansea. She had visited Tiverton, Rhode Island, and Dartmouth, Massachusetts, by 1779. No records of her itineraries for this period have been discovered, but it is certain that she was traveling almost constantly and that gradually others not of her family found validity in her religious teachings and joined in fellowship with her to form the nucleus of an identifiable sect.

Chapter II

Saith the Universal Friend

THE times were auspicious for religious novelty, as the established political, economic, and social order of life crumbled in the turmoil of the American Revolution. Not only was Rhode Island in the forefront of the pre-Revolutionary protests against British colonial regulations, but it was one of the first colonies to send troops to Boston after the outbreak of hostilities in the spring of 1775, and, as a state, was affected directly by military action or occupation for most of the succeeding years of the war. From December, 1776, when the British occupied Newport, until October 1, 1779, when they left, American forces were stationed in the state to prevent a more general invasion. After the British evacuated Newport, the town became the headquarters for the French fleet and French troops from July, 1780, to March, 1781. Thus Rhode Island was an armed camp, held by foes, friends, or allies, for most of the war.

Jemima Wilkinson began her ministry just as the influence of the war began to be felt sharply in Rhode Island. For the next six critical years of the American Revolution, she traveled in and around Rhode Island, virtually ignoring the political and military conflict and its issues. As the Publick Universal Friend she spoke of her own war against sin, to soldiers, both American and British, to refugees and prisoners, and to patriots and loyalist sympathizers alike. She was able to avoid identification with either side in the struggle for independence; those who joined her included former soldiers in the Revolutionary forces, Tories, and many who were pacifists during the war.

The earliest account of Jemima Wilkinson's ministry, preserved with the Wilkinson papers, was written by Ruth Prichard, a follower and one of the principal scribes of the Universal Friend:

The Friend of Sinners began to serve In the year 1777 When this Nation was still in arms and America had embroiled her hands in human blood. There appeared the Messenger of Peace going from City to City and from Village to Village proclaiming the News of Salvation to all that would Repent and believe the Gospel. The Friend was not staid by guards of armed men. She went through to visit the poor condemned prisoners in their Chains. Naked swords shook over the Friend's head, she was not in terror because of the mighty Power of the Lord. No storms or severity of weather could hinder the Friend's journey to speak unto Souls like the un-wearied Sun, Determin'd its faithful race to run, spreading heavenly benediction far abroad that wandering sinners might return to God. And Travelling far & wide to spread the glad tidings & news of Salvation to a lost and perishing & dying World who have all gone astray like Lost Sheep;—The Lord has lifted up his Hand To the Gentiles and set his Hand the Second Time to recover the remnant of the lost Sheep of the House of Israel. He that hath ears to hear, let him hear.

Among those who heard were the American soldiers stationed in the towns that Jemima Wilkinson visited in the first year or two of her ministry. Keeping an eye on the British in Newport was a dull job, so these men undoubtedly were delighted with the diversion of a good-looking female preacher. Even General Horatio Gates was in the audience at one of her sermons. She was per-mitted to visit prisons and to speak with prisoners, and she would travel long distances to attend the executions of persons condemned as spies. On these occasions and at funerals, which she attended at every opportunity, she emphasized the transient nature of life and the neces-sity of repentance. "Large assemblies" were attracted to hear her wherever she went. It was unusual enough, out-side of the Quaker meetings, for a woman to be preaching at all, but Jemima Wilkinson was distinguished by her claim that she was restored from the dead to bring her message. Rumors and elaborations extended the stories beyond her actual claims, so that her appearance anywhere was sure to attract a crowd of curious onlookers. Abner Brownell, one of her early followers, noted, "The Manner, Appearance and Method of her coming forth as a Preacher different from all other Sects or Denominations of People, being a Woman of extraordinary natural Abilities, of a Gift in Speaking as an Orator, and a great Memory of the Scriptures, that there has Abundance of strange Reports spread abroad concerning her, some false and some true, which produces Abundance of Spectators and Enquirers."

The sensation she caused was in part due to the popular belief, expressed by President Manning of Rhode Island College (later Brown University), that she "pretended to be Jesus Christ in the form of a Woman." As Ezra Stiles heard the story, "she died & is no more Jemima Wilkinson. But upon her Restoration, which was sudden, the person of Jesus Christ came forth & now appears in her body with all the miraculous Powers of the Messiah." This allegation, which was widespread, stimulated much of the hostility against Jemima Wilkinson and led to frequent charges of blasphemy. As far as can be determined, Jemima was careful never to make this claim herself in any public speech. Soon after she began to preach, and before she left her home in Cumberland, she made a straightforward denial of the story in the presence of Moses Brown. Ezra Stiles reported also that she told the Reverend Eales of Stonington that when she called herself the Comforter she did not mean that she was the Holy Ghost, but one raised up by God to give comfort to His people. Several of her followers made public denials of the persistent charge that the Friend had Messianic pretensions, a charge especially resented by those who settled with her in western New York. A local historian, who collected information from surviving followers and their descendants fifty years after her death, classified this as "derogatory and scandalous stuff" and stated flatly,

"She never claimed to be a Messiah nor a substitute for a Messiah, but simply a minister of truth sent by divine authority to preach a better life to the world."

The answer to the confusion seems to be that Jemima Wilkinson was many things to many people. Her mysticism was more strongly emphasized in the early years of her ministry than after she settled in New York State, but from the beginning to the end of her life she described her mission in ambiguous terms. In a letter written in her defense after her death, "A Neighbor" remarked:

A report has long been current that she professed to be the *Messiah*, at his second coming, *to gather the elect, &c.* To questions calculated to draw out from her satisfactory evidence on this point, I could never obtain any other answer than a string of scripture quotations, and visions of her own seeing: calculated, however, to encourage the belief that she acted by immediate inspiration.

It was charged that this ambiguity was designed to encourage those who were willing to believe her to be divine and not to offend those who thought of her only as an expositor of religious verities.

The religious teachings of the Universal Friend were an interesting blend of practical, familiar biblical axioms and obscure mysticism involving interpretation of dreams, prophecies, and faith healing. Faith healing, associated with the early years of her ministry, was abandoned before she moved to Pennsylvania and New York. Prophecies and interpretation of dreams continued to the end of her life. The Wilkinson papers include page after page of accounts of dreams, carefully written out in minute detail for the Universal Friend by her followers. Of course such mysticism did not appeal to all her adherents, many

of whom followed her because they believed in the truth
of her moral and spiritual teaching. Acknowledgment of
her spiritual leadership, however, meant acceptance of
her interpretation of her call—that Jemima Wilkinson was
dead and that the Universal Friend was a new spirit
sent by God to use her body. Brownell described her
account of her divine commission as given in one of
her sermons:

> She will exhort them much to be sure they do not reject
> the counsel she delivers, and speaks much of unbelief . . . that
> unbelief shuts people out of the kingdom of heaven, and that
> if they do not believe . . . they will be in the state of the
> unbelieving jews, who rejected the counsel of God against
> themselves, and will tell them that now is the eleventh hour,
> and this is the last call of mercy that ever they will have, for
> she heard an enquiry in heaven, saying, "Who will go and
> preach to a dying world?" or words to that import, and she
> says, she answer'd and said, "here I am, send me [see Isaiah
> 6:8]," and that she left the realms of light and of glory, and the
> company of the heavenly host that are continually praising
> and worshiping of God, to step down here upon his footstool,
> to be trodden under foot by the children of men, and to go
> through many sufferings and trials, and afflictions, and hard-
> ships, which she will enumerate and tell over.

Jemima Wilkinson evidently had some sort of messianic
complex that helped to create a sublime self-confidence,
which, with her evident sincerity, contributed to her
effectiveness as a preacher. The very audacity of the
implications in her sermons impressed many in her audiences, for, as Brownell observed, "no Person would
rationally think, that any Person in their right Senses, would
dare to hold forth and affirm such great and exalted

Things concerning themselves, and to have such a great
and marvelous Mission, and to hold forth nothing but
what they had immediately by divine Revelation, unless
it was so in Reality." It does not seem credible that she
could have played the role she did with such success
unless captivated by an unfeigned obsession. The unlet-
tered farm girl from the back-country town of Cumberland faced audiences, large and small, with complete
assurance and poise. She delivered her message in
crowded city churches and to single families in isolated
frontier cabins, before foreign nobility, learned scholars,
soldiers, Indians, farmers, men and women of all social
classes and from all walks of life. It was not Jemima Wilkinson who spoke, she maintained, but the spirit of the
Publick Universal Friend, using the body of Jemima
Wilkinson to carry out a divinely appointed mission.

It was, from all accounts, an attractive body indeed.
Jemima Wilkinson was about medium height for a woman,
with a fine figure; "well made" was the eighteenth-
century expression. Her eyes were dark and expressive
and her features regular. Glossy black hair hung in ringlets
to her shoulders, a feminine touch to her masculine
costume and appearance. The Marquis de Barbé-Marbois,
who devoted enough time to American women in his
travels to be considered something of an expert on the
subject, described her as he saw her in Philadelphia:

This soul sent from heaven has chosen a rather beautiful
body for its dwelling, and many living ladies would not be
unwilling to inhabit that outer shell. Jemima Wilkinson, or
rather the woman whom we call by that name, is about
twenty-two years old [she was actually almost thirty]. She
parts her hair on top of her head, and lets it fall onto her

shoulders. Her only care for it is to wash it every day in fresh water; she never powders it. She has beautiful features, a fine mouth, and animated eyes. Her travels have tanned her a little. She has a melancholy and thoughtful air, and no cultivated charm, but every charm that nature gives. She carries herself easily and freely, and at the same time with all imaginable modesty. She has a large gray felt hat with turned up edges, and she lays it on the desk of her pulpit when she preaches. She wears a kind of cloth smock tied under her chin like a dressing gown. It falls to the feet, without outlining her figure, and its sleeves reveal only the tips of her hands.

Others were less lyrical, but all the descriptions of her as a young woman agree that she had much natural beauty. Even a bitterly critical essayist described her as "about the middle size of woman, not genteel in her person, and rather awkward in her carriage, her complexion good, her eyes black, and remarkably brilliant, her hair black, and waving in beautiful ringlets, upon her neck and shoulders, her features regular, and the whole of her face thought by many to be perfectly beautiful." Another saw her as "straight, well made," with "light Complexion, black Eyes, round face, chestnut dark Hair."

With instinctive showmanship, Jemima Wilkinson set off her physical beauty by an unusual and original costume. It is not clear when she adopted the garb that became an identifying feature, but at least as early as 1778 her person was described as "something singular and extraordinary, appearing in a different habit from what is common among Women, wearing her hair curl'd in her Neck, without any other covering on her Head, except it was when she travel'd out, she put on a Hat much like a Man's, only the Brim flap'd down." The attention her uncovered head attracted should be explained by recalling that no woman in that day was considered properly dressed without her cap. An uncovered head indoors was a male prerogative.

Her clothing emphasized her masculine appearance. It most resembled the gowns worn by the regular clergy in the pulpit. She usually wore loosely flowing black robes with a man's white kerchief or cravat around her neck. Sometimes this garment was white or even purple. In New Haven in 1787 she wore a "light cloth Cloke with a Cape like a Man's—Purple Gown, long sleeves to Wristbands—Mans shirt down to the Hands with Neckband—purple handkerchief or Neckcloth tied around the neck like a man's—No Cap—Hair combed turned over & not long—wears a Watch—Man's Hat." The hat was similar to that commonly worn by Quaker men. It was usually of white beaver with a flat crown and broad brim, which she tied down with a kerchief when she traveled. This costume gave her a decidedly clerical air, emphasizing the role of preacher to which she felt she had been called. "Her head is dressed like that of a man and she has the look of one," commented an observer in 1788; "her shirt was buttoned close under chin and sleeves close to the wrist, with a black gown, such as church ministers wear, from shoulders down to her feet." The masculine impression encouraged by her dress was strengthened by the fact that her associates never referred to her in the third person but always as the Friend.

Her voice was described as "very grum and shrill for a woman" by one witness and as "masculine" by another. When she visited Philadelphia, her Rhode Island accent, evidence of her Yankee heritage, was noticed. Her pronunciation was in "the peculiar dialect of the most illiterate of the country people of New-England," according

to one hostile observer. Jacob Hiltzheimer, a Pennsylvania
Dutchman, reported simply, "Her speech was much in
the New England dialect." Her voice did not diminish her
effectiveness as a speaker, however. According to Moses
Brown, she had "a fair Countenance, a Good Voice of
Utterance, and Captivating powers of oratory." Another
description of her manner of speaking noted: "In her
public address, she would rise up and stand perfectly
still for a minute or more, then proceed with a slow and
distinct enunciation. She spoke with great ease, and with
increased fluency; her voice clear and harmonious, and
manner persuasive and emphatic." In 1828, a writer who
called himself "Lang Syne" remembered seeing her when
he was a schoolboy in Philadelphia:

She appeared beautifully erect, and tall for a woman, although at the same time the masculine appearance predomi-
nated; which together with her strange habit caused every eye
to be rivetted upon her. Her glossy black hair was parted
evenly on her pale round forehead, and smoothed back beyond the ears, from whence it fell in profusion about her
neck and shoulders, seemingly without art or contrivance—
arched black eyebrows and fierce looking black eyes, darting
here and there with penetrating glances throughout the assembly, as though she read the thoughts of people; beautiful
aqueline nose, handsome mouth and chin, all supported by a
neck conformable to a line of beauty and proportion; . . .
she spoke deliberately, not "startling and rash," but resting
with one hand on the banister before her, and using but occasional action with the other, nevertheless she seemed as one
moved by that "prophetic fury" which "sewed the web,"
while she stood uttering words of wondrous import, with a
masculine-feminine tone of voice, or kind of croak, unearthly
and sepulchral.

The Universal Friend always spoke extemporaneously, in the Quaker manner, "as the spirit moved her." Since the spirit sometimes moved her to speak for several hours, it is no wonder that her sermons seemed to lack organization and, occasionally, even coherence. "Her preaching has but little connexion," Brownell noted, and she was "frequently very lengthy, standing at times for several hours, sometimes cold and languid, but at other times it is said she is lively and discovers . . . zeal and animation." The sermons were based on scriptural texts. The texts of her sermons, carefully noted in the journals and diaries, cover a variety of subjects in both the Old and the New Testaments. The variety of texts, however, according to Brownell was not greatly significant:

After she has taken a text, she never expounds or explains much upon it, but leaves it as abstruse as it was before, and then goes on mainly to set forth what she calls the present dispensation, and that what she delivers is divine counsel, as she knows nothing of herself, she will say, but as her heavenly father reveals: so she speaks, unto a dying world, and so she will generally entertain people with a long discourse, in which will be many entertaining and necessary instructions that are very applicable.

Jemima Wilkinson's success in attracting followers was proof of her effectiveness as a speaker, but the secret of her power to move people evidently was not in what she said, which was apt to be "commonplaces from the Bible," nor even in the manner of her speaking, but in the absolute self-confidence and evident sincerity with which she spoke. Brownell explained, "She exhorts in a pathetic Manner, with great Confidence and Boldness, and Confirmation of her being right, and all others being

wrong; says that she has an immediate Revelation for
all she delivers." This belief that what she spoke came
to her directly from God was, of course, an important
legacy of her Quaker heritage.

The Publick Universal Friend developed no new doctrines or tenets, no original theology or elaborate polity.
In fact, she avoided the doctrinal points that were the
basis of much sectarian dispute and preached a message
of simple morality, illustrated by familiar biblical stories,
expressed in scriptural language. Many of the principles
and practices she advocated were either actual duplication
or slight modifications of old-fashioned Quaker beliefs,
although the influence of her association with the New
Lights is evident also. She stressed the imminence of
millennial judgment and described with great effectiveness
the punishments that awaited the sinful. "She Preaches
up Terror very alarming," noted one observer.

Considering the novelty of the circumstances and manner of her preaching, the contents of the sermons of
the Universal Friend were surprisingly commonplace.
President Ezra Stiles of Yale modified a first, unfavorable
impression of her, based on hearsay, after he heard her
speak in New Haven in 1787. She "preached or discoursed in the grave, tonic & unconnected Manner of
the Friends or Quakers. . . . She said many pious good
Things & Exhort[a] to Virtue, with many Texts repeated
without Connexion," he reported, and concluded with the
opinion that she was "decent & graceful & grave."
Another observer, who heard her near Philadelphia in
1788, recorded with some surprise, "From common
report I expected to hear something out of the way in
doctrine, which is not the case, in fact heard nothing

but what is common among preachers, and commendable." One of her early followers described her discourses as containing an "Abundance of scripture Expressions, though not much explain'd or Light held up from them; neither did I ever hear her advance much scripture Doctrine of the Principles of Religion . . . but her Exhortation seemed to be very effecting, and she shewing a very sedate Countenance of Solemnity and Seriousness, and admonishing all to repent and forsake Evil, and learn to do well, and live as they would wish to die."

The simplicity of the ideas in her sermons was reflected in her letters. She wrote to John and Orpha Rose in 1789:

Dear Souls, Try to make your escape from the Wrath which is to come, upon all the wicked, that no not God; & have not obey'd the voice of the dear Son of His Love: It is a Sifting time; Try to be on the Lords side; Do justly love Mercy, and walk humbly with the Lord: . . . Do all of you try to obey the Counsil of the Lord which ye have heard from time to time: That it may be well unto you: Do by all as ye would be willing to be done unto: . . . Saith the Friend.

Repent and forsake evil, prepare for a future judgment, and obey the simple morality of the Golden Rule was the essence of her message.

It could hardly be expected that a young woman of limited experience, with no formal education, whose only religious training was her own study of the Bible and a few books of Quaker theology and history, would develop a religious system with a strong intellectual appeal. But for many the emotional impact of her personality, strengthened by the aura of mysticism that surrounded her, opened new insight and gave new meanings to the familiar biblical texts and stories that she recited.

Ruth Prichard, a lifelong follower of the Universal Friend, explained her feelings in 1786, shortly after her conversion:

I was sincerely a Seeker; and did not mean to mock the Sacred Name. . . . But dear Soul, we must seek before we can find, we must knock before it will be open unto us. While I was thus a lost Enquirer, and as I was then must never have seen the Smiling Face of Jesus; Lo! The Universal Friend was to pass thro' Wallingford where I kept school: And I with some more went on First Day, (hearing the Friend was to Preach at such a House) about 7 Miles to hear. And blessed be the day I went; O! Blessed be the Lord for giving me this great Day of visitation: And I do testify unto Thee, my dear Friend it was the Voice that spake as never Man Spake. It is that which if obey'd will bring Light Life & Love unto the Soul; That peace that the world can neither give nor take away. And there is nothing below the Sun shall tempt me back, the Lord helping me.

An earlier convert, Abner Brownell, first heard of the Universal Friend in 1778 and journeyed to Tiverton, Rhode Island, to hear her speak. He noticed that many of her adherents appeared

very devout in their Worship, of much Humility and of Prostration, and Appearance of much Reformation, of which they and she said they were some of them turn'd from the most loose and vain Lives of almost any People, now to a Life of Virtue and Piety, and abandoning all evil Vices and Practices. . . . Thus her Doctrine and Practice of Performance in Religion, seem'd to have so much Resemblance of Holiness and the Truth, and so much favourable Expectation to the natural Man, that that would answer for to embrace, as the Religion which is after Godliness, that after I had heard several Times I was much engaged to have Unity and Fellowship with it.

For nearly three years Brownell was an active follower of the Universal Friend, traveling with her and visiting other members of her society on her behalf. He did not record his observations and impressions until after he had broken with her over the issue of a book explaining his own religious philosophy, which he had published without first obtaining the permission of the Universal Friend. The tone of Brownell's small book about Jemima Wilkinson is neither especially bitter nor excessively hostile, but is decidedly critical and probably reflects the bias that might be expected of an estranged follower. Brownell describes her method, saying that once the Universal Friend has made a successful first impression on people "by Degrees she will unfold to them mysterious Things concerning herself, what she says she has met with, and how great a Work she is sent upon, and what Revelations and Visions she has; and as they begin to listen to these Things, and as she finds they will receive it, she will go from step to step as it were, discovering to them concerning herself, sometimes very plain, and then deliver something more mystical, if she finds they do not digest that." Her purpose, Brownell charged, was to make herself "the object of their faith."

Some of the women who followed Jemima Wilkinson did seem to revere her with an adoration that was close to worship. Sarah Niles ended a note to the Universal Friend containing Sarah's interpretations of some chapters from Revelation with the statement, "I do believe the power is sufficient to cause the dumb to speak, the deaf to hear & the dead to be raised." "I desire with all the remainder of my Days, to devote to Thee. I would follow no other voice but Thine," wrote Ruth Prichard

Spencer to the Universal Friend. Mehitable Smith explained
in a letter to Orpha Rose, "how much better then to
suffer afflictions with the followers of the holy one then
to injoy the pleasures of the world and have its aplause
and ly down in everlasting Sorrow when time is don." In
spite of the personal loyalty and devotion that she
attracted, and a firm conviction that her words as the
Universal Friend were divinely inspired, Jemima Wilkinson did not assert any claims to personal divinity. The
role she performed was that of a spiritual guide, an
interpreter of the will of God, a heavenly messenger. As
a group of her followers meeting in East Greenwich,
Rhode Island, in 1783 expressed it, she was "the one
who is the means in the hand of the father of Mercys
in leading us to the fountain of liveing waters flowing
freely through our Dear Redeemer Lord & Saver Jesus
Christ."

Not all the methods that she used in attempting to
impress people were above criticism. Brownell charged
that she collected information from her followers and
other persons and used it to convince the faithful that
nothing could be hidden from her. He also revealed an
incident in which he was persuaded to copy sections
from certain books and have them published as a book
in the name of the Universal Friend. Unlike other of
his allegations, this can be checked and is, indeed, true.
A book entitled *Some Considerations, Propounded to the
Several Sorts and Sects of Professors of This Age* . . .
by "a Universal Friend to all Mankind," attributed to
Jemima Wilkinson, was printed by John Carter of Providence in August 1779. An examination of the text shows
that the entire text is copied almost verbatim from the

Works of Isaac Penington, the Quaker preacher and writer, and from William Sewel's history of the Quakers. A few words are changed here and there, such as making Friends read United Friends, but the work is clearly a plagiarism. It was done, as Abner Brownell explained, at the request of Jemima Wilkinson, who convinced him that the thoughts were "applicable to the present dispensation" and would have the greatest effect if published in the name of the Universal Friend. When Moses Brown saw the book at the printer's office and recognized it as selections from Penington's *Works*, he was told by one of Jemima Wilkinson's followers, "Could not the Spirit dictate to her the Same Word as it did to Isaac?" In spite of this exposure, the book had a limited circulation among the followers of the Universal Friend in Rhode Island, where it was generally accepted as her own writing.

That these excerpts from standard Quaker sources could circulate as Jemima Wilkinson's ideas indicates how similar were her religious teachings to basic Quaker beliefs. This was evident even to contemporary believers. Brownell observed that her doctrine was, "as to the general tenor of it, much (as to the principle part) in resemblance of the ancient Friends, or Quakers, so called, as you may observe in Robert Barclay's apology." Like Barclay, Jemima Wilkinson rejected the Calvinist doctrines of predestination and election. Her preaching was based on an assumption that the individual had freedom of will to choose between good and evil and that Christ's death was an atonement for all who would accept him. She seems simply to have accepted this position, and a belief in the Trinity, as consistent with her understanding of the Bible, her primary source, without attempting to explore the theological subtleties involved. Although, as one of her followers explained, "The Friend endeavored always to expound religious doctrine in perfect harmony with the Bible," all her religious teachings were based on the faith that God speaks directly to the human spirit. His message could come through intuition, dreams, visions, or through some appointed messenger such as the prophets of old, or the Publick Universal Friend. While orthodox Quakerism, with its fundamental emphasis on the "Inner Light" in each person, also put great responsibility on the individual, it sought the truth not in the expression of a single person's interpretation of God's will but in the prayerful consideration of what was manifested to all the individuals in the group. Jemima Wilkinson's heresy to the Quakers was, as William Savery expressed it, "the exalted character she gave to her own mission," which "savoured strongly of pride and ambition to distinguish herself from the rest of mankind, by the appellation of the Universal Friend."

Even her new name, Publick Universal Friend, was Quaker in origin and implication. Public Friends were members of the Society of Friends who felt a concern or call to preach and were authorized to travel from meeting to meeting for that purpose. Jemima Wilkinson simply added the word Universal, implying a broader mission. The very concept of a new name for a reborn spirit reflected Quaker acceptance of Isaiah's affirmation (Isaiah 62:2): "Thou shalt be called by a new name which the mouth of the Lord shall name." Having been to heaven, as she maintained, the new spirit in her body must take its new name. Officially the Publick Universal

Friend, she was called also the Universal Friend of Friends, the Friend to all Mankind, the All-Friend, the Best-Friend, or, most commonly, simply The Friend.

Many, if not most, of the individuals who joined Jemima Wilkinson came from Quaker backgrounds. Attending her meetings, however, was considered a cause of stumbling for orthodox Quakers. Jeremiah Browning of Hopkinton, Rhode Island, was taken under dealing in August, 1780, for attending two such meetings near the Friend's Meeting House in Hopkinton. He was forgiven after writing a letter of contrition which read:

> Whereas I did some time past attend two meetings of Jemima Wilkinson on the same day that Friends meetings were held where I used to attend all which being Contrary to the good Order Established among Friends I therefore Condemn the Same and Desire Friends to pass it by and continue their watchfull care over me. To the Mo^{ly}. meeting of Fr^{ds}. to be held at So. Kingstown 25th of ye 9th mo 1780.

Externally there was little to distinguish one of Jemima Wilkinson's society from a member of the Society of Friends. Most of her followers followed her admonition to wear plain apparel with no ornamentation and to use the *thee* and *thou* of the plain language. Like the Quakers they rejected the "heathen names" for the days and months, designating the date according to the number of the day and month. The Publick Universal Friend and her society followed Quaker practice in not observing or recognizing as sacraments any ceremonies such as baptism or communion, in standing firm against war and violence, and in opposing Negro slavery. The meetings appointed by the Universal Friend, little different in theory from regular Quaker worship, were gatherings to

await the Holy Spirit to move someone to speak. As in
Quaker meetings the men wore their hats. Sometimes the
meeting passed in silence; at other times members of the
group spoke or offered prayers. Whenever Jemima Wilkinson herself was present, she was moved to give a
sermon, usually lasting an hour or more. Meetings were
concluded by everyone's shaking hands according to the
Quaker custom.

Although Jemima Wilkinson achieved considerable fame,
or notoriety, even in the earliest years of her ministry,
she was not subjected to mob attack or physical violence
such as was directed against Ann Lee and John Murray,
the two religious innovators with whom she was most
commonly compared. Perhaps it was because her religious
message lacked the originality that led to the establishment of the Shakers and the Universalists in America.
Then too, Jemima Wilkinson was a native-born American,
supported by many whose loyalty to the American cause,
in that time of bitter conflict, was unquestioned. Ann
Lee was often accused of being a British spy, and her
opposition to war and violence was misconstrued as a
plot to aid in the reconquest of the colonies. Jemima
Wilkinson attracted persons of greater wealth and higher
social position than those who became Shakers. As Robert
St. John pointed out, "In this respect Jemima Wilkinson
is distinguished from Ann Lee and the general run of
New England enthusiasts. The latter gained converts
chiefly from among the ignorant and the credulous; but
the Friend was able to convince the most practical and
intelligent of her fitness for spiritual leadership." Brownell
observed in 1782 that "some wise and learned Men of
great Parts have been attached to her . . . as well as

many ignorant and illiterate People that are ready to be carried about with every Wind of Doctrine." Few converts of either category joined the fellowship of the Universal Friend in the first two years of her ministry, however, although her public meetings were crowded. Her headquarters was still the Wilkinson family farmhouse in Cumberland and her only financial support was her father's bounty and the simple hospitality she received in the homes of her few supporters. The road for a woman who felt herself called to the exalted position of nondenominational evangelist in eighteenth-century New England was not an easy one.

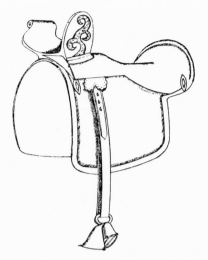

Chapter III

Refuge in Little Rest

THE Publick Universal Friend decided to carry her
message to England. It was an audacious project for the
twenty-six-year-old woman, but two years of almost constant speaking before greatly diverse groups must have
given her the fluency and confidence that comes with
experience. Although her own faith in her commission
was unshaken, she may have been discouraged at the
uncertain prospects of convincing her fellow countrymen
of her divine mission. So, with few followers and little
financial support, in the fall of 1778 Jemima Wilkinson
experienced what was called "a Strong Apprehension in
her Mind, that for the Good of Mankind, She is Divinely
called to go and preach to the people in England."

Calling on General John Sullivan, commander of the American forces in Rhode Island, she had no difficulty in getting his permission to pass through his lines to British-occupied Newport "in order to Take a Passage from thence to England." Jemima's sister, Marcy, and Rhoda Scott of Bellingham, Massachusetts, were also permitted to go, but a request to have William Aldrich of Smithfield accompany them caused some difficulty. General Sullivan was reluctant to allow a young man of military age to pass under British jurisdiction without some special authorization. William Aldrich, who later married Marcy Wilkinson, then petitioned the General Assembly of Rhode Island to allow him to make the trip with the women. He pleaded that he usually attended "the Meetings of the People called Friends" and had taken the affirmation prescribed by law for "Persons of tender Consciences, against the Art of War and Fighting, and the Use and Exercise of Arms." The petition was granted without comment by the lower house on October 30, 1778, but evidently in the upper house it aroused some suspicions. On November first, permission for the voyage was granted with the condition that after reaching the island of Rhode Island, on which Newport was located, the four were not to return to any of the United States within three years, under a penalty of being apprehended and tried by court martial as spies. Fortunately for the Universal Friend's plans, this condition was reconsidered and the petition finally granted, subject only to such restrictions as General Sullivan might prescribe.[1]

Jemima Wilkinson did visit British-occupied Newport, and there preached against "sin, war, and fighting." It was reported that, hearing the British asperse the rebels, "she told them publickly in the streets that those they called Rebels were not so great rebels only against an Earthly King, they against the great King of Heaven." The mission to England did not materialize. Perhaps the British authorities thought they were plagued enough with troubles from the colonies without accepting a Yankee female who claimed to be a reborn spirit returned from the dead, and refused permission for the voyage. It is also possible that Jemima Wilkinson changed her plans, or received divine instructions superceding her first call. It is clear that after November, 1778, her fortunes took a decided turn for the better. About that time she met Judge William Potter of South Kingstown and his family, and made converts of them. Judge Potter was one of the wealthy, slave-holding Narragansett planter aristocracy, and, by marriage to a distant cousin, Penelope Hazard, was allied with the prolific and distinguished Hazard family. His share of the Potter lands, inherited from his father, Colonel John Potter, included what was known as the Homestead Farm, about a mile up North Road from the village of Little Rest. Judge Potter put his spacious home at the disposal of the Publick Universal Friend and, thus provided for, she moved the center of her operations from Cumberland to Little Rest. The projected journey to England was not mentioned again.

Jemima Wilkinson's first visit to South Kingstown was recorded by Daniel Updike, who noted in his diary for November 15, 1778; "Went to the Hill to hear Miss Wilkinson preach who I liked very well." Two days later he again went to the Hill to hear her preach and reported that "the Galeries like to have fell the post underneath giving Way by Slipping." The Hill probably was Tower Hill, where both the Quaker meeting house and the Congregational church were located, but it could have been Little Rest Hill. The village of Little Rest, whose name was changed to Kingston in 1825, was the administrative center of the Town of South Kingstown and the county seat of King's (later Washington) County. The county courthouse there was one of five places in which the General Assembly of the State of Rhode Island met periodically. Jemima Wilkinson was certainly in Little Rest by the spring of 1779, when "Nailer Tom" Hazard went to hear her at Thomas Champlin's after dining at William Potter's on March 2, 1779.

Judge William Potter was fifty-seven years old in 1779, and the father of thirteen children, the oldest of whom was a year older than Jemima herself. His household five years earlier consisted of twenty-seven persons, including eleven Negro slaves. Distinguished in the records from others of the same name by designation as William Potter, Esquire, he had begun a career in politics—befitting one of his wealth and social distinction—soon after he was admitted a freeman in 1744 at the age of twenty-one. He served in several town offices, acting as town clerk of South Kingstown for more than two decades and representing the town in the colonial legislature on several occasions, both as Deputy in the lower house and as an Assistant in the upper house. In 1768 he was elected by the legislature to the first of several terms as Chief Justice of the five-man Court of Common Pleas for King's County. His political career was threatened on the eve of the Revolution, in April, 1775, when as a member of the upper house he joined with the Governor, the Lieutenant Governor, and another Assistant in dissenting from a resolution of the General Assembly to raise an army of observation. The Governor, Joseph Wanton, a staunch defender of colonial rights,

who balked at armed resistance to the British government, was eventually deposed. With the political acumen
acquired by long experience, Judge Potter soon recognized
that his participation in the dissent threatened to end his
public service. In a petition to the General Assembly
he showed himself to be a master of hyperbole as he
protested his loyalty to the patriot cause.

No man hath ever been more deeply impressed with the
calamities to which America is reduced, by a most corrupt
administration, than myself. No man hath more exerted himself
in private and public life, to relieve ourselves from our op-
pressions; and no man hath held himself more ready to sacrifice his life and fortune in the arduous struggles now making
throughout America, for the preservation of our just rights
and liberties; and in these sentiments, I am determined to live
and die.

Sorry I am, if any of the good people of this colony should
have conceived otherwise of me; and I greatly lament, that the
unguarded expressions in that protest, should give cause there-
for. Should I from thence, lose the confidence, just hopes and
expectations of my countrymen, of my future conduct in the
arduous American struggles, it might create an uneasiness of
mind, for which nothing can ever compensate.

But should this public declaration ease the minds of friends,
and the friends of liberty, and convince them of my readiness
to embark, to conflict with them in every difficulty, and
against every opposition, until our glorious cause shall be established upon the most firm and permanent basis, it will be a
consideration that will afford me the highest satisfaction that
human nature is capable of enjoying.

Squire Potter's petition was accepted by the legislature,
which soon afterwards re-elected him as Chief Justice of
the Court of Common Pleas for King's County. He supported the cause of independence faithfully throughout

the war until 1779, when his political career ended abruptly as he became a convert of Jemima Wilkinson, the Publick Universal Friend. It is possible that the Judge resigned from the various offices he held when he joined with the Publick Universal Friend, but no resignations can be found in either the state or town records. It is more likely that he simply was not re-elected when his association with such an unorthodox religious figure became known.[2]

Ezra Stiles visited Little Rest in September, 1779, and talked with Judge Potter. Most of the information he recorded in his diary, however, was a report from someone else who interviewed one of the daughters, Alice Potter Hazard, wife of Captain Arnold Hazard and daughter-in-law of a former Lieutenant Governor of Rhode Island. Mrs. Hazard was a loyal follower of Jemima Wilkinson all her life, but nothing in later years confirmed the relationship described by Stiles.

In her prayers she addresses the public Friend whom she says is omnipresent, & calls her *Messiah* & herself her *Prophet* —she says Jemima is the *son of G^d* and *the Messiah reappear^g* in flesh; *the son of G^d whom the Father hath put to Death;* that whosoever shall believe on Jemima shall be saved but whoever shall not believe that Jemima or the Public Univ. Friend is Jesus Christ the Savior, and herself his Prophet shall be everlastingly damned. That the Univ. friend has anointed her (Alice Haz^d) to be a prophet, and accord^y she predicts the day of Judg^t to come in half a year. The Prophet began to think and be concerned last Spring (1779) & began to prophecy beginning of Sept. or 3 Weeks ago. That Jemima has ordained 12 Disciples and is to come into Narraganset again.

In view of later developments this characterization, which

Stiles based, not upon observation, but on hearsay, cannot be true, but it does represent the sort of story that was told and believed about Jemima Wilkinson and her followers. Stiles, who at that time had not met Jemima, believed that she was suffering from a "temporary Insanity or Lunacy, or Dementia quoad hoc." He also thought that Mrs. Hazard was undergoing a "Fit of Lunacy or Insanity," and reported that her mother, Mrs. Potter "had a season of Distraction," and that a son, aged seventeen, was taken insane and raving last spring and put in chains. This last reference seems to be to William Robinson Potter, who did not live to adulthood. He was probably the young man whom Jemima Wilkinson treated for insanity, with some temporary success. The decision of the Potter family to follow the teachings of the Publick Universal Friend, however, cannot be explained satisfactorily by calling them insane. Nor, as was slyly insinuated, could a sexual attraction of Judge William Potter for Jemima be the answer.

The women of the Potter family, including Mrs. William Potter, accepted the Universal Friend and her faith with a more abiding loyalty than the men. Penelope Hazard Potter was raised as a Quaker and used the plain language, as did her daughter, Alice Potter Hazard. Undoubtedly the Quaker background was a factor in attracting them to the Universal Friend, but their life-long allegiance must have been based on a real conviction in the validity of her religious teachings. Penelope Hazard Potter was more loyal to Jemima Wilkinson than was her husband, continuing in the faith of the Universal Friend after Judge Potter defected. Spencer Hall, the last surviving follower of the Universal Friend in Rhode Island, wrote to Rachel and Margaret Malin in 1827 that he had seen Mrs. Potter shortly before her death and she had told him she meant to live and die a Friend.

Association with the Publick Universal Friend involved the whole Potter family. The eldest son, Thomas Hazard Potter, married Jemima's sister, Patience Wilkinson, seven years his senior. Benedict Arnold Potter, after the Revolution known as Arnold, left Harvard College to join the Universal Friend and, incidentally, to begin a courtship that led to his marriage with Sarah Brown, one of Jemima's most loyal companions. Penelope Potter married Benjamin Brown, Jr., Sarah's brother, also a member of the Universal Friend's society.

The influence of the Universal Friend was evidenced in other ways. Jemima Wilkinson opposed the practice of slavery; the Universal Friend's society had no color bar. Although Judge Potter depended upon slave labor to farm his acres, he began to free some of his slaves soon after joining the fellowship. In certificates of manumission dated March 27, 1780, he gave freedom to two of his slaves, Mingo and Caesar. The witnesses were other members of the Universal Friend's society, Abner Brownell and Sarah Negus.[3]

The most tangible evidence of the Potter family's new religious affiliation was a fourteen-room addition that Judge Potter had built on to his already spacious mansion to house Jemima, her retinue, and the guests who came to visit her. Probably her public meetings were also held there. Even after she left Little Rest, the building on North Road, known as the Abbey, or the Jemima Place, stood for years as a reminder of the prophetess and stimulated the retelling of the various stories about her that were part of the local lore.⁴ Her name was also perpetuated by the local name for a species of solidago, or September weed, called Jemima weed because it appeared there about the time she first came to the neighborhood.

When Jemima Wilkinson first moved to Little Rest, she seemed to have felt that the millennium was imminent. According to Abner Brownell, she predicted the fulfillment of the prophecy of Daniel (12:11, 12) and of Revelation (11:2; 12:6) to begin "something in the first of April, 1780, being about forty-two months after her first beginning to preach, which was not so fully and plainly held forth by her as by some of her Apostles; but the time expired and nothing happen'd: a while after on the 19th of May was the dark day, and then she made application of that's being the fulfilling of her prediction and what was to happen, and so that doctrine seem'd to die away, and there wasn't much said about it afterwards, only it would be in the Lord's own time, &c."

The Dark Day, mentioned by Brownell, was one of the most unusual natural phenomena of the whole colonial period in southern New England. For several days before the mysterious event the atmosphere was smoky, but on the nineteenth of May, 1780, at about ten in the morning, the sun was blotted out and it became as dark as night. The strange darkness was not an eclipse of the sun. Combined with a smoky smell and copper red or yellow clouds, it lasted until about two o'clock in the afternoon and was a terrifying experience for many. The event is recorded in many diaries and journals and in the newspapers of the day, and for a generation people remembered and spoke of the Dark Day with awe.⁵

It would not be surprising if Jemima Wilkinson, who accepted the prophecies of the Old Testament and the allegories of Revelation as literal truths and to whom visions and dreams represented the unfolding of the divine will, found this extraordinary occurrence significant. By a remarkable coincidence this day also marked a tragic event in the life of Jemima Wilkinson and of the Potter family, with whom she now made her home.

Susannah Potter, the lovely twenty-two-year-old daughter of Judge William and Penelope Potter, died on the nineteenth of May, 1780. The Death Book of the society recorded, "She died in the Arms of the Friend." Jeffrey Watson wrote in his diary the only extant contemporary reference to this tragedy. "Susannah Potter Daughtir to Wm Potter Esqr Dyed the 19 of May about 8 in the morning and was buried the 22 Day of May 1780 the publick friend preached her funiral Sermon to a very large orditory." Another detail which cannot be confirmed by any documentary evidence was included by Wilkins Updike in a book published in 1847:

Susannah Potter, a daughter of the Judge, having deceased, she [Jemima] undertook to raise her to life. On the day of the funeral, a great concourse assembled to witness the miracle. The lid of the coffin was removed, and Jemima knelt in devout and fervent prayer for her restoration. The laws of nature were unflexible. The impious effort was unavailing. She imputed the failure to the old excuse, the want of faith in her followers.

This bit of folklore, which first appeared in print nearly seventy years after the event supposedly happened, must be suspect, although the coincidence of Susannah Potter's death and the strange happenings of the Dark Day make such an attempt a possibility. Abner Brownell, writing in 1782, described Jemima Wilkinson's activities in great detail, including "her Prophesies, and foretelling of future Events and pretended Gift of Healing." He mentioned the Dark Day but had nothing to say about any attempt to raise Susannah Potter from the dead, an incident, had it happened, that could not have failed to attract his attention and would certainly have been recorded in his account.

All the attempts at faith healing by Jemima Wilkinson are related to the early years of her ministry in New England. In describing her methods of "Healing of People," Abner Brownell wrote:

She would tell them if they had Faith to believe, why she could do it, but if at any Time any Body made Application to her and was not heal'd, she said it was because they had not Faith; but several People who were got in a spleeny, histeric Way, and remain'd a good while in a low State, being a good Deal discouraged, and she having them immediately taken up, and to stir and ride about, it would seem to make a sudden Alteration with them, and they would get pretty well soon, and then there would be a great Report of a Miracle's being done, which would be much nois'd abroad.

Some cases, such as those who were "very poor in a consumptive way" and did not have the strength to be moved about so, did not live long, Brownell reported. Ezra Stiles recorded in 1779 an incident that he "had from one present":

Lately at Dighton Jemima began the miracle of heal^g the sick, a woman long confined to her bed by Infirmities. A comp^a gathered—Jemima raised the Woman (who had great faith in her) from off her bed & led her across the room which she had not done long before. But when the Miracle had proceeded thus far Mrs Dagget a noisy religionist began a warm Dispute with Jemima, & she left the Miracle unfinished and poor Mrs.____Limbs are as fixt as ever & she returned to her Confinem^t in bed.

Evidently Jemima Wilkinson abandoned the practice of faith healing before she left Rhode Island. No accounts of any such incidents in Pennsylvania or in New York State are recorded, although the Universal Friend had a reputation as a skilled frontier practitioner, setting broken bones and doctoring the Genesee fever and other illnesses with medicines and folk remedies. Mystic though she was, Jemima Wilkinson never denied the existence of sickness or of bodily death. In fact, death seemed to be much on her mind and was stressed in her sermons, although she emphasized the immortality of the soul. She declared, according to Brownell, that "she was as much prepared the moment she enter'd the world to leave it again, and go to the innumerable host of angels, as she should be if she was to live here a thousand years, and says that she lives every day as if it was the last, and will say . . . that she should be glad if it was the will of God to call her out of the world before the light of another day." Most of her letters contained the phrase, "The Friend is yet in time." The phrase "left time" was the expression used by the Universal Friend and her society to refer to death. The attraction of the Universal Friend was certainly based on more than a naïve belief that she had power to perform miracles or tell fortunes.

After 1779 more and more men and women joined in fellowship with Jemima Wilkinson to form a loosely organized society. Later in her career she surrounded her-

self with women and gave the highest positions of authority and trust in her society to members of her own sex.
In these early years, however, her principal advisers were
men. Next to Judge William Potter in importance was
Captain James Parker, also of South Kingstown.[6] Parker
was a landowner and justice of the peace. When military
forces were first raised at the beginning of the Revolution, he was quick to volunteer his services, although
his mother was a Quaker preacher and opposed to
bearing arms. He was one of the original members of
the Kingston Reds, formed in October, 1775, and later
joined the regular military forces, reaching the rank of
captain. In May, 1779, he resigned as captain in Colonel
Crary's regiment, and devoted his efforts to the cause of
the Publick Universal Friend. Another Revolutionary
soldier and member of the Kingston Reds was John
Rose, who with his wife Orpha became important members of the Universal Friend's society.[7] Another South
Kingstown member was John Reynolds, known as
Jemima's John to distinguish him from others of the same
name in his prolific family.

Another center of support for the Universal Friend in
Rhode Island was East Greenwich. Here members of
the Nichols, Briggs, Hall, Spencer, and Wall families were
active followers, and here a meetinghouse was built for
her. An acre of land was given by John and Mary Nichols
in September, 1783, and held in trust for the society by
Peleg Briggs, Robert Hall, and George Spencer. The latter
was known locally as Jemima's George. One of the
numerous Spencer clan poked fun at this George with
the comment that he would "as soon worship a *Wooden
God* as a *Woman God*," a quip that caused considerable

local amusement. The meetinghouse was built, a simple, plain, one-story building, about four miles southwest of the village of East Greenwich in the section of town called Frenchtown.[8]

This first acquisition of property by the followers of Jemima Wilkinson made some form of organization imperative. At a meeting held in East Greenwich on September 18, 1783, the trustees named above were chosen, and a public statement was drawn up. Describing her work, it stated:

The Publick Universal friend of Friends . . . hath for several years past Laboured among us with Unwaryed Pains in Preaching the Everlasting gospel in Publick Congregations of People & in private familys in visiting the sick & Prisoners by night & by Day by whose seasonable Instructions admonitions & Invitations in the Demonstrations of the Spirit & with power (haveing estemed the most spotless & Unblemished Character) Numbers of People among us have been brought out of the Kingdom of Darkness into the Kingdom of God . . . we own and acknowledge that it was by obeying the Divine Counsil Spoken to us by & through the Dear Universal friend of friends that we are redeemed from wrath to come & are brought into Union with God & his holy one & have & are incorporated into a Religeous Body or Society of People who call our Selves & are known by the name of Universal Friends.

The deed transferring the land for the meetinghouse also repeated the name of the society as the Universal Friends, "being under the Particular care and direction of a Person known to them by the Name and distinction of the Universal Friend." Three years before, when the book *Some Considerations* was printed in Providence, the name used was the United Friends, and in a letter to Abner Brownell, dated the 30th of the 8th month, 1782, Mehitable Smith wrote, "I am in Union with . . . the Brethren of the United Friends in Jesus Christ in which Church we both profess to belong." After 1783, however, the name Universal Friends appeared whenever a reference was made to the society.

Jemima Wilkinson was a frequent visitor to East Greenwich. On one occasion she was holding a meeting in a farmhouse about a mile and a half west of the village. In the midst of her talk she paused for two or three minutes and then spoke, "It is made known to me and handed down from the Father of Mercies from above that there is some one within the sound of my voice that will not live to see the light of another day." That night an aged Negro who lived in the house died.[9]

For some nine years, from the fall of 1778 to the fall of 1787, South Kingstown was the center of Jemima Wilkinson's activities. Not only was Judge William Potter's comfortable home available to her, but many other families of followers lived nearby, and it was a central location for the journeys that carried her from New Bedford, Massachusetts, on the east to New Milford, Connecticut, on the west, with additional trips across New Jersey to Philadelphia. The Universal Friend and her entourage on the road made an imposing sight. The procession seldom contained less than a dozen riders strung out two by two with the Universal Friend at the head of the column, stately and erect in her sidesaddle. She loved a fine, spirited horse and took pains that the animals in her company received the best care. Often at her side, in the place of honor, rode distinguished old Judge William Potter. Young Tom Hathaway sometimes rode beside her,

taking care to keep the head of his horse not quite
even with hers. This position he earned as a lad of sixteen by rescuing the Universal Friend when her horse
bolted. This woman, dressed in flowing white or black
robes, with a broad-brimmed beaver hat tied down over
her long black curls, was a sight to stop and look at, and,
once seen, was not forgotten. The Reverend John Pitman
encountered the procession while on his way to Pawtuxet
on September 22, 1783, and wrote, "Saw Jemimy Wil-
kerson the Imposter with the number of Deluded Crea-
tures that go about with her standing &c in the Road
about 4½ Miles from Providence." Her procession probably served the same purpose as a circus parade. It could
hardly fail to attract attention, arouse curiosity, cause
discussion, and draw a crowd to the meetings appointed
by the Universal Friend.

The general attitude toward Jemima Wilkinson was apt
to be one of decided hostility. Even in her naitve Rhode
Island most people knew of her only from hearsay and
formed their opinions from the exaggerated stories that
depicted an unscrupulous, immoral, blasphemous woman
who sought to exploit a few deluded followers by pre-
posterous claims of supernatural powers. When she
appeared in person, however, Jemima Wilkinson generally
overcame the popular prejudice against her. Those persons
who heard her speak or engaged her in private conversation usually thought favorably of her. Many who would
not join her followers became her friends. Among these
was Stephen Hopkins, first cousin of Jemima Wilkinson's
father and Rhode Island's most distinguished citizen.
Nominally a Quaker, although disowned for his role in
supporting the war for independence, he was a man whose

religious views approached deism. Jemima Wilkinson often visited him, it is said, and was always "courteously received and kindly conversed with." A story has survived that when Stephen Hopkins was so seriously ill, just before his death, that no visitors were permitted, Jemima Wilkinson called several times and insisted that she be allowed to see him. At last her request was sent up to him, "but his answer is not remembered." It is unlikely that the Universal Friend had her final opportunity to try to save the soul of her distinguished kinsman, who died in 1785, but as long as he was able he treated her with respect.

She was also welcomed as a guest in the hospitable home of Dr. Joshua Babcock of Westerly. A graduate of Yale and a physician trained in Boston and London, Dr. Babcock served in both houses of the Rhode Island legislature and was Chief Justice of the Supreme Court. He was an active supporter of the Revolution, serving as a major general in the State Militia and as a member of the Council of War. Not only was Jemima entertained at his home as she passed through Westerly on her travels but she even held meetings there. Perhaps, as has been suggested, this consideration was out of friendship for Judge William Potter, but it also illustrated Dr. Babcock's own independence in religious matters. Described as "generous and catholic in his Charity & Benev° toward all Xian Sects . . . [he] would occasionally attend all kinds of Worship with not only freedom & Decency, but sincere Devotion." It is unlikely that men of the position and experience of Babcock and Hopkins, inclined toward skepticism of all forms of revealed religion, would have spent time listening to Jemima Wilkinson unless they were impressed by her sincerity or by her personality.

Most remarkable of all is the fact that the self-taught farm girl could feel at ease visiting homes where Washington and Franklin had been honored guests.

Perhaps living with the aristocratic Potters taught the young prophetess some of the social amenities that she needed to match the zeal born with her vision. Certainly the first few years after the Publick Universal Friend found a refuge in the Potter mansion, north of Little Rest, were important ones in the development of her religious society. Until 1782 most of the friends and supporters of the Universal Friend were Rhode Islanders. After that date, however, other New Englanders were enlisted, and her parish was extended, even to Pennsylvania.

Chapter IV

New England Ministry

FROM her native Rhode Island, the Publick Universal Friend gradually extended her parish to include all southern New England. In the dozen years after she began to preach until she finally left New England, Jemima Wilkinson traveled almost constantly, seeking new converts and sustaining the zeal of the avowed members of her society. Several important centers of support developed as individuals and whole families from eastern Massachusetts to western Connecticut accepted her religious leadership. By 1789, her society had attracted sufficient attention to be included in the list of recognized religious denominations of Rhode Island published in

Jedidiah Morse's pioneer text, *The American Geography*. "A small number of universal friends, the disciples of Jemima Wilkinson," was listed with the Baptists, Friends or Quakers, Episcopalians, Moravians, Jews, and a considerable number of "Nothingarians."

The Universal Friend had little success in her initial forays outside Rhode Island in southeastern Massachusetts. She may have gone as far as Boston on her early preaching excursions, but the only evidence of her activities in this region is an undated sermon, found among her papers, entitled "An Answer to Roxbury People." In this sermon she warned about "Dangerous Curiosity."

Be not Curious to Search into the Secrets of god   Pick not the Lock where he hath allowed no key   he that will be fitting every Cloud may be smitten with a thunder Bolt he that will Be too familiar with gods Secrets may Be overwhelmed with his judgements   Adam would Curiously increase his knowledge wherefore Adam Shamefully Lost his goodness   the Bethshemites would needs pry into the Ark of god therefore the hand of god Slew above forty thousand of them, therefore hover not above this flame Lest you Scorch your wings   for my part I will Carefully improve myself By what we have reveald and not Curiously inquire into or after what he hath Reserved

The "Book of Conscience" was the next topic.

Wouldst thou know whether thy name be written in the Book of life, Why then read what thou hast written in the Book of Conscience, thou needest not Ask who Shall Ascend up into heaven for to Search the record of Eternity, thou mayest But Descend down into thine own heart and there read what thou art and what thou Shalt Be; tho gods Book of Election and Reprobation Be Closed and kept above with god yet the Book of Conscience that is open and kept Below in thy very Bosom, and what thou writest here, thou Shalt Be sure to read there, if you write nothing in this Book but the black Lines of Sin, you will find nothing in gods Book but the red Lines of damnation, but if you write gods word in the Book of Conscience, you may be Sure god hath written your name in the Book of Life at the great day of judgement when all Books Shall be opened there you will Either read the Sweetest or the Sharpest Lines   I will therefore so write here that I may not Be ashamed to read hereafter

About "Death," she wrote:

Nothing is So Sure as death and nothing so uncertain as the time when we may be too old to Live   We can never be too young to Die   I will therefore Live Every hour as if I were to die the next—

The theme of death was carried into the next section, "As We Live So We Die."

That way the tree inclineeth while it groweth that way it picheth when it falleth and there it Lieth   who [?]eth whether it be North or South   as we are in Life for the most part we are in death   So we Lie down to Eternity whether it Be towards heaven or towards hell   Being Once fallen there is no removing   for as in war an Error is death So in death an Error is damnation   therefore Live as you intend to die and die as you intend to Live   O Lord let the Bent of my Soul be always towards thee and ever rest with thee—

She concluded with an admonition:

As to the Vain inquiry that is made Concerning the Universal Friend   I desire to Speak in Love and I must Say that I Look upon it neither descent nor honorable But rather

an imposition and I Cannot give an answer   it is what I do
not know   the Counsel is that if Obeyed Brings peace to
my Soul   So far as I have Obeyed the words that are
Spoken they are Spirit and they are Life   it is the Spirit
that Quickeneth   the flesh and Blood profiteth nothing

Although her words were far from startling, the fact
of a woman preaching at all was unorthodox enough to
arouse opposition. Jemima Wilkinson made few converts
in the homeland of the Puritans. One outstanding addition
to her society, however, was the Hathaway family of
New Bedford. The Universal Friend visited Dartmouth
and the New Bedford area early in her ministry. James
Hathaway became a follower as early as 1779. More
important, however, was his brother, Thomas Hathaway, Sr., a wealthy shipbuilder. Thomas Hathaway was a
staunch Tory, who fled New Bedford at the beginning
of the Revolution and lived with his father-in-law in
Nova Scotia for six years, serving on a British man-of-
war for more than a year of this time. His wife and
four children were left behind in a country home near
New Bedford to try to hold on to the family property.
In spite of his pro-British role, Thomas Hathaway seems
to have returned home after the war without difficulty.
He joined the Universal Friend soon after his return,
was one of the party that accompanied her to Philadelphia
in October, 1782, and remained a loyal and active leader
of her society until his death, the only former Tory prominent in the group.

Connecticut proved to be a more fruitful field for the
Publick Universal Friend than Massachusetts. Converts
were won in several towns across the state; in the
Stonington—Groton—New London region and in the vicin-

ity of New Milford she was especially successful. The Stonington–Groton–New London area was near enough to her headquarters in Little Rest so converts could make frequent pilgrimages there and she could join them regularly for religious services. Orthodox Quakers from Groton and Stonington worshiped at the Hopkinton, Rhode Island, meetinghouse, built nearly on the Connecticut line, and were under the discipline of the South Kingstown monthly meeting. When Jemima Wilkinson began to hold meetings in Hopkinton in 1780, the Society of Friends warned its members not to attend and disciplined any who did. This did not deter Richard Smith of Groton and his son and daughter, Richard, Jr., and Mehitable. Richard Smith was an outspoken man who sent what was termed "one of the earliest documents against slavery in New England" to the South Kingstown monthly meeting about 1757.[1] Disowned by the Quakers for his attentions to the Publick Universal Friend, Smith and his son became important members of her society and Mehitable Smith, one of Jemima Wilkinson's most loyal adherents.

The largest addition to the Universal Friend's society from southern Connecticut consisted of the five sons of Benjamin Brown, of Fisher's Island and New London, and their families. Benjamin Brown the elder died before 1782, leaving five farms to be divided among his ten children. Of these children, Benjamin, Daniel, James, Elijah, and Micajah were followers of Jemima Wilkinson, as were a number of the children of Benjamin, Daniel, and James. Jedidiah Holmes and his family, of Stonington, and Latham Avery, of Groton, were other members of the society from this area.

New Milford, on the Housatonic River in western Connecticut, was also a center of the Universal Friend's society, second only in importance to South Kingstown, Rhode Island. Jemima Wilkinson first visited New Milford about 1782 and found a welcome in the homes of several families in the northern part of the town and in the adjoining town of Washington. Members of the Dayton, Botsford, Stone, Barnes, Ingraham, and Dains families were some of the "persons of very honorable and Christian character" who joined the New Milford society of Universal Friends. The number of converts soon made a meetinghouse necessary, and in June, 1784, Abraham Dayton deeded a piece of land to the society for that purpose, and "for the promotion of the Cause of God, and the advancement of the true Church and Kingdom of Jesus Christ . . . [and] for the Increase and propogation of the everlasting Gospel of Jesus Christ amongst the Children of men." The land was held in the name of Asahel and Benjamin Stone and Jonathan Botsford, Jr., three trustees of the "Society of people who call themselves and are known by the name Universal Friends." A small building was constructed about four and a half miles north of the village of New Milford, adjoining the burying place in the Northville section of the town.[2] After the Universal Friend extended her influence to the vicinity of Philadelphia, New Milford became important as a central location for the Rhode Island and Pennsylvania followers.

Jemima Wilkinson was probably en route to New Milford in 1785 when the schoolteacher Ruth Prichard heard her in Wallingford and joined her as a scribe and keeper of the society's Death Book, a record of the dates when members in good standing "left time." At about

the same period Jemima Wilkinson met Sarah Richards
and her husband, Abraham, of Watertown, Connecticut.
Sarah's marriage was not a happy one. After her husband
died in 1786 while on a visit to Jemima Wilkinson in
Rhode Island, the young woman and her infant daughter,
Eliza, joined the Universal Friend's household. Sarah
Richard's father was Dr. Henry Skilton, a wealthy physician who practiced in several Connecticut towns and at
one time owned a store, a hotel, a mill, and two or
three farms. Although she was five years younger than
the Universal Friend, the two women became the closest
friends, and soon Sarah Friend, as she was called, was
recognized as a religious leader in the society, second
only to the Universal Friend herself.

Sarah Friend embarked on preaching missions and was
sent to take charge of proselytes in one section of the
country when the Universal Friend had to be in another.
She too had visions, which were especially impressive
because they were accompanied by the epileptic trances
to which she was subject. In her manner of dress and
appearance she followed the example of Jemima Wilkinson. A description in 1787 noted that she "appears
to be about twenty-eight years of age [actually she was
only twenty-one], is sensible, and would be a comely
person, were she to dress as becomes her sex. But as
she imitates the person they call the friend, in her external
appearance, and particularly in wearing her hair down
like a man, she is by that means somewhat disfigured."
Utterly devoted to her leader, Sarah Richards willingly
sacrificed comfort and companionship with her baby
daughter to serve the Universal Friend. Sharper of tongue
than Jemima and without the Universal Friend's ability

to charm and to win over persons with opposing views, the younger woman was more practical and, in spite of her youth, came to act as a sort of business manager for the Universal Friend, holding property in her name in trust for the Universal Friend.

As the Publick Universal Friend, Jemima Wilkinson remained aloof from temporal concerns. She received no regular salary as a minister, for the society never had sufficient organization to have a common treasury out of which she could be supported. Since she began her ministry without a penny of her own and received nothing from her father or from his estate, she was dependent upon gifts from her supporters. A popular belief that she requisitioned what she needed with the command, "The Lord hath need of that," was always strongly denied by her followers and others who knew her well. Brownell recorded concerning gifts to her: "She will tell them if the heart is with the gift or offering, she can accept it." The expenses of her travels and her clothing, specially made and always of the finest material, were provided for her by her followers, and other free-will offerings supplied her with such luxuries as silverware monogrammed with the initials U. F., a fine leather and velvet sidesaddle with silver stirrups, special china and pewter, and furniture. These personal possessions she considered her own, but she never held any real property in her own name. The meetinghouses in East Greenwich and New Milford were held in the name of the society by boards of trustees.

With no real organization to bind the members of her society, the Publick Universal Friend spent much of her time in traveling. Although occasionally it was necessary to spend an evening at a public inn, usually the Universal Friend was a guest in the home of one of her followers or in the home of some friend or acquaintance. Sometimes she was invited to visit with people who had heard about her and were curious to meet her. Young Thomas Hathaway, who accompanied Jemima on trips across Connecticut, noted in his journal, "Many of the most respectable people came from different parts of the state to invite her to their neighborhood and homes and it seemed to be with us as with the Disciples in breaking of bread from house to house in singleness of mind."

Wherever she happened to be, in a public house or in a private home, she held a meeting or a sitting. It might be a silent meeting, a simple sitting with spontaneous testimonies, or a full-scale meeting in which the Friend preached from a text. Benedict Robinson's diary, kept on a trip from Judge William Potter's home in Little Rest across New England en route to Worcester, Pennsylvania, in November, 1787, noted the meetings held each day of the journey. On the first Sunday, November 18, the Universal Friend held a meeting in the home of Jedidiah Holmes in Stonington, at which she preached from Isaiah 44:3-5. The meeting "was wonderfully attended with Divine love and power of Holiness and Purity, and offers and invitation handed forth to the audience." The next three days were spent at Benjamin Brown's in Groton. At the "sittings" held there in the evening, "sinners were invited and exhorted to obedience," "the audience entreated to obedience and love," and "exhorted to humiliation and repentance." All across the state of Connecticut, the Universal Friend concluded her day of travel on horseback with an evening sitting such as the one at a tavern in East Guilford, where she "exhorted to humiliation and prayer and a daily walking with the Lord and a state of Watchfulness." Sometimes the evening sittings were silent; but on other occasions the Universal Friend or others in the party spoke, with "much being said." Once the Friend spoke to the company at breakfast and then had another meeting in the evening of the same day.

Traveling almost constantly as she did, Jemima Wilkinson visited the homes of her followers at fairly regular intervals. Such a visit was a great event that called for the finest hospitality the family could offer. Brownell suggested that the Universal Friend was served because of a superstitious awe of her supposed supernatural powers. The letters and journals of her adherents indicate, however, that she was regarded with real love and affection and that the women, especially, delighted to serve her with the best they could offer.

She never traveled alone and usually had from six to a dozen companions on a journey. Seldom could one home house the entire company, so the Universal Friend and one or two of the women customarily stayed with one family while the others lodged in various nearby houses. Upon arriving, everyone shook hands by way of greeting, and the Universal Friend was shown to a private room, unusual in that day when it was not uncommon for several travelers to share a single bed, with others often occupying the floor of the same room. Jemima seemed to cherish her privacy and almost always ate alone in her room with the door closed. Sometimes one or two of her closest companions joined her for a meal. She usually had two or three women help her to get dressed and to change her clothes. The Universal Friend was much more concerned with cleanliness than was customary in that time. Her habit of washing daily was strange enough to attract attention and even suspicion, and her desire for clean clothing was regarded by some critics as almost sinister. "She must have fine holland," it was reported, "and to shift her cloaths almost every day, to keep them clean and white, which is business enough to employ one person or more to wash and iron for her." Willing attendants were never hard to find, and the women who traveled with her and the women of the household where she was a guest competed for the honor of serving her.

As did most traveling clergymen, the Universal Friend repaid the hospitality shown her by holding worship services. But she was also considered a source for advice on all manner of subjects. The women asked her about their cooking, how to make their clothes, and other domestic problems. The men brought her questions about their business and even sought advice on farming. She was also a mediator in the disagreements among members of her society. On March 16, 1785, a diary recorded: "The Friend had Daniel Brown & son Daniel & Jedediah Holmes together before a number of friends in order to settle some old difficulties which had subsisted some time. Dan¹ & son said they would settle & be satisfied could they see a reformation in Jedᵃ." Jedidiah's comments on this occasion were not recorded.

Naturally, traveling as they did from one end of New England to the other and visiting in one another's homes, the various families that shared a common religious faith in the Universal Friend's society became well acquainted.

Younger members of these families met other young people from distant towns, fell in love, and got married. Four of Jemima Wilkinson's sisters, her earliest converts, married members of the society. Thus the Wilkinsons of Cumberland were allied with the Potters of South Kingstown and the Botsfords of New Milford. Potters married Browns from Groton, and Botsfords married Hathaways from New Bedford. Eventually all of the leading families in the society of Universal Friends were linked together by ties of marriage.

The number of marriages and the children that resulted from them seem to be a tangible contradiction of the doctrine of celibacy taught by the Universal Friend. The answer lies in a careful analysis of what she taught on the subject. In her printed advice and in her public lectures she dealt with the subject with characteristic ambiguity, and although she probably was more specific in private conferences, she did not make direct public prohibitions of marriage or sexual relations. Her feelings about sex seem to be based on a literal acceptance of Paul's teachings on the subject in Romans 8:6-18, I Corinthians 7, and Galatians 5:16–17. Like Paul, she felt celibacy was a higher state of grace, which she intended to practice herself and to urge upon members of her society. She agreed with Paul, however, that "it is better to marry than to burn" and did not prohibit marriage or insist that husbands and wives live apart. In fact, most of her followers were married couples who continued to live together under the same roof. The children who were born from time to time were evidence of the occasional triumph of the demands of the flesh. No one was expelled from the society for such lapses or for marrying.

Celibates were more highly regarded by the Universal Friend than were married couples. A number of unmarried and widowed women, later described as the Faithful Sisterhood, and even a few men did practice celibacy. The Universal Friend attempted to discourage marriage when she could. Benajah Botsford, who wished to marry her younger sister, Deborah, was exiled to Nova Scotia for three years before they finally were married. When Ruth Prichard entered into what proved to be a very unhappy marriage with a man outside the society, she remained close to the Universal Friend and continued to keep the society's Death Book until a few months before she died. The persistent charge that Jemima Wilkinson caused many families to be broken up is hard to substantiate with specific examples. Some husbands may have deserted their wives, and some wives may have left their husbands. Probably some individuals used her teachings as an excuse to escape unpleasant domestic or conjugal responsibilities. This persistent impression, however, in both Rhode Island and Connecticut, that Jemima Wilkinson was responsible for many broken homes, was an important factor in arousing public opinion against her in these areas.

Jemima Wilkinson's leniency in enforcing celibacy upon her followers is in sharp contrast to the practices of her contemporary female religious leader, Mother Ann Lee, of the Shakers. The Shakers insisted on the separation of couples and enforced strict segregation of the sexes. Without equivocation, Ann Lee was proclaimed the Elect Lady, the female embodiment of Christ, a more exalted role than that claimed by Jemima. It is highly unlikely that Mother Ann exerted any influence on Jemima Wilkinson.

Although she arrived in New York City in August, 1774, two years before Jemima's vision, Ann Lee worked in quiet anonymity as a domestic until the spring of 1776, when she founded her colony at Niskayuna, near Albany, New York. The Shaking Quakers were getting in the harvest of their first crop when Jemima Wilkinson experienced her vision and began her ministry as the Publick Universal Friend in far-off Rhode Island. By the time the Shakers began active proselyting in 1780, Jemima had already collected a group of followers and had achieved considerable fame in southern New England. The similarities between the two women more likely stem from their common debt to Quakerism than from any contacts with each other.

It is inconceivable, however, that these two women, each carrying out what she conceived to be a divine mission, should have been unaware of each other. For three or four years before her death in September, 1784, Ann Lee preached her gospel through western Massachusetts and as far east as Harvard and Shirley, at the same time that Jemima Wilkinson was also traveling in southern New England. But the paths of the two women never crossed, and no early contact between any of their followers is recorded. Evidently, Ann Lee made no real attempt to carry her mission into Rhode Island or southern Connecticut, while the Publick Universal Friend seemed to avoid central and western Massachusetts, and the northern Hudson valley. Some of the followers of each could have been attracted to the other, but, with the outstanding exceptions of some of the Baptist clergy, Shaker converts tended to be people of humble circumstances, poor farmers scrabbling for a living on a few

acres of stony Berkshire land, bound girls, or hired hands.
In contrast, the majority of Universal Friends were people
of some wealth and social position in their community.
The requirements of the Shakers were more specific and
difficult and thus more challenging. It took considerable
sacrifice to accept the enforced celibacy, public confession, dancing, shaking, speaking in unknown tongues, and
other practices of the Shakers; the teachings of the Universal Friend seemed almost prosaic in comparison.

In the public mind, however, the two women were
often compared, and perhaps sometimes confused. President James Manning of Rhode Island College, in his
letters to England after the war, included Jemima Wilkinson, Ann Lee, and John Murray among the afflictions
suffered during the Revolution. Ezra Stiles compared the
two women in a lecture at Yale in February, 1781.
Jemima Wilkinson was mentioned in the earliest popular
account of the Shakers, a small book by Valentine Rathbun, a Baptist minister of Pittsfield, Massachusetts, and
a former Shaker convert. First printed in Providence in
1781, it appeared in eight editions between 1781 and
1783 and reached a wide audience.[3] In the introduction
to the first edition, Rathbun warned:

There never was a day that more loudly called for careful
watchmen, than the present time; while we see Satan trans-
forming himself into an angel of light, and bringing forward
his deep laid scheme, to undermine the glorious plan of redemption by Christ: And as he first deceived the woman, and
use of her to delude the man; so he is playing his old prank
over again, sending one woman from the State of New York,
and another from the State of Rhode Island (Jemima Wilkinson) who vie with other, and are as dangerous to the heedless

passengers, as Scylla and Charybodes are to the unskilful
mariner.

Jemima Wilkinson must have known of Rathbun's
book. A note preserved in her papers, dated the eleventh
month, 1781, and labeled "Vision of Dream of M. T.,"
described an experience of one of her admirers.

Being at a friend's house on a Visit there was handed to me
Book Set out by one Rathbone about a sett of people at or
near alboney   Having read the Book my mind was much
staid upon the auther of all things and my spirit drawn out
with ardent Desire to god In the Name of Jesus the savour
of the world that if I had favour With the Father of spirits
that he might Revele to me what these two Persons were that
caused so much talk in the world. I went to bead, and it
pleased God to shew me in the Vission of the Night, Two
lights in the form of two full moons about one hower High
in the west, one of them had the face of the son of God in it
And the other was a plane moon.

M. T., who addressed the account of her vision "For
the Universal Friend," obviously identified the moon
bearing the face of God with Jemima Wilkinson and the
plain moon with Ann Lee.

Jemima Wilkinson herself was the subject of a book
published in 1782, the year after Rathbun's first appeared.
Abner Brownell's *Enthusiastical Errors, Transpired and
Detected* was mentioned earlier. Its format indicates that
he may have been attempting to pattern his account of
Jemima and her sect after Rathbun's popular exposé of
the Shakers. In his introduction Brownell claimed that
he had seen and heard "the leaders and Chief teachers"
of both the Shakers and the Universalists as well as the
Universal Friend. He did not once use the name Jemima

Wilkinson, however, in any of the forty-four pages in the book, but referred to her as "an anonymous Person, who gives herself the Title of 'The Universal Friend.'" Brownell's book lacked the bite and sensationalism of Rathbun's often-reprinted volume and evidently had a rather limited circulation. It reached a number of people interested in religious activities, however, and was cited on several occasions.

By 1784, Jemima Wilkinson was sufficiently well known to be included in the first edition of Hannah Adams' *An Alphabetical Compendium of the Various Sects*, an important reference work that was republished in 1791 and 1801 as *A View of Religions*. The paragraph about Jemima Wilkinson was based largely on Brownell's account. Volume II of Isaac Backus' pioneering work on the Baptists, *A Church History of New-England*, published in Providence in 1784, also contained a quotation from Brownell's book as well as some observations of his own about Jemima Wilkinson. In his opinion, "her influence has not been half so great and extensive as that of [Ann Lee]."

It is difficult to compare the two women. Ann Lee laid the foundation for a more durable and more significant religious organization than did Jemima Wilkinson, but its development was largely due to others and came after Mother Ann's death. In death Mother Ann Lee became a symbol to the Shakers. Her memory was used by other able leaders in building the complex religious, economic, and social system that became the Shaker way of life. Jemima Wilkinson failed to attract any associates trained in philosophy or theology or original enough to develop a distinctly different religious system. She was

more reactionary than radical, stressing the fundamentals
gleaned from her study of the Bible and her understanding of ancient Quaker practices and principles. With
no fixed doctrines and no formal organization, her personality became the primary attraction and her will the
ultimate authority within the society. By 1787 she had
attracted a following of at least two hundred people from
about forty families, mostly in New England.

From New England, the Publick Universal Friend carried her message to Pennsylvania. She was on her way
to Pennsylvania in 1787 when she spoke before an audience of about three hundred persons in New Haven, on
Sunday, November 25. Here President Ezra Stiles of Yale
met her for the first time. As the meeting began, Jemima
Wilkinson was seated with her companion in chairs on
the upper step of the Court House. First, she kneeled
and prayed and then stood and preached for about an
hour, taking as her text Isaiah 55:6 and 7. Latham
Avery then spoke for three or four minutes, after which
the Universal Friend spoke again, and then again; then
kneeled and prayed and wished a blessing. Benedict
Robinson noted that a few in the audience "paid a serious attention to what was said but the greater part was
a wild and unstable company." Ezra Stiles spoke with her
after the service, and his daughters visited her at Elias
Shipman's house, where she was invited for tea later
in the afternoon. The Universal Friend declined an invitation to breakfast with the Stiles family, sending a note.
Stiles's impression of Jemima Wilkinson after he met her
was much more favorable than his earlier comments
about her, based on hearsay. When Jemima passed
through New Haven again a year later, she did not call

on Stiles, who heard of her sojourn in town only after she left. She was returning from a year in Pennsylvania, full of plans to go to the Genesee country, where, as she reported, her friends had already purchased a large tract of land on which they could settle together.

This was her third visit to Pennsylvania. She had stayed in Philadelphia first for a few weeks in October, 1782, and attracted considerable attention. Her next trip included not only Philadelphia, but also nearby Worcester in Montgomery County, and part of New Jersey—a tour lasting in all from August to October, 1784. Probably she spent the winter of 1784-1785 at New Milford, returning to Judge Potter's mansion at Little Rest in March, 1785. Plans for a separate community of Universal Friends began to be formed in 1785. Explorations were made in the Genesee country of western New York in the winter of 1785-1786. As the plans to settle in western New York progressed, the Friend shifted her headquarters from New England to Worcester, Pennsylvania, where she spent the year from November, 1787, to November, 1788. The winter of 1788-1789 was her last in her native New England. Many of her New England followers were already in the new settlement when she left South Kingstown for Worcester, which she reached in February, 1789. Jemima Wilkinson was in her thirty-seventh year when, for the last time, she left the stone walls and wooden houses of her native New England for the stone houses and wooden fences of Pennsylvania.

Chapter V

Pennsylvania

THE Publick Universal Friend first set out from Little Rest for Philadelphia in the fall of 1782. The fighting in the American Revolution was over, and for all practical purposes had been since Cornwallis surrendered at Yorktown, an event duly celebrated in Little Rest by firing cannons on October 27, 1781, ten days after the event took place. For six years of the war, Jemima Wilkinson had carried on her own campaign across southern New England, ignoring the military struggle and its issues. Now, with the arrival of peace, she proposed to carry her message to the largest urban center of the new United States, a city whose Quaker heritage would naturally attract the young prophetess.

Nothing she had yet experienced could prepare the Universal Friend for Philadelphia, described before the war as the second largest city in the British empire, surpassed only by London itself. The birthplace of American independence, which had been the seat of government of the new nation except during the British occupation of 1777-1778, was again the nation's capital. With a cosmopolitan population of over twenty thousand persons, only half of its prewar number, Philadelphia was still much larger than Boston or Newport, both of which the Friend had seen under extraordinary wartime conditions, and it completely dwarfed such familiar places as Providence, New London, New Haven, and New Bedford. Accompanying Jemima Wilkinson on this expedition to Philadelphia were Judge William Potter, his daughter Alice Hazard and son Benedict Arnold Potter, Sarah Brown, Thomas Hathaway, and William Turpin. The route they took was probably through the central Connecticut towns of Windham, Andover, Bolton, East Hartford, Farmington, and Litchfield to New Milford, over the Hudson at Newburgh, and down across New Jersey to Philadelphia.

Philadelphia was the scene of Jemima Wilkinson's greatest triumphs as a preacher and of the most bitter attacks she had ever received. She and her small band rode into the city in October, 1782, without a friend and not knowing where they would lay their heads at night. Although Judge Potter had served in the legislature with three of Rhode Island's delegates to Congress, such old acquaintances were apt to be cool or openly unfriendly since he had abandoned politics for the service of the Publick Universal Friend. Even in cosmopolitan Philadelphia the costumes worn by Jemima and her women

companions attracted unfavorable attention, and stories
of her pretensions aroused opposition. Their troubles were
described in a report dated February 23, 1787, published
in *The American Museum.*

In the fall of the year in 1782, it was rumoured that a singular
female preacher with two other women, and four men as
companions, were arrived in this city, in order, as it was said,
to publish and declare the glad tidings of salvation, and that
the day of the Lord was near to be revealed. But as the wom-
en's dresses were singular or uncommon, it was with difficulty
they could procure entertainment; yet at last it was obtained,
at a widow's in Elfrith's alley, whose heart and house were
open to their reception. Next morning, two friends, who had
been at one of their meetings, gave forth a report of the awful-
ness of the solemnity with the innocent yet majestic appearance of the woman preacher, that they were struck with
wonder and amazement by her preaching and praying, which
were wholly in the method of friends or quakers. Thus her
behaviour, conduct, and appearance soon sounded abroad; and
on the succeeding evening an unruly company assembling, it
was thought prudent to keep the doors and windows shut,
there being apprehension of personal insults from the liberties
taken by boys, &c. A dreadful scene of outrage ensued; stones,
brick-bats, &c. were thrown against the house; which was contrary to the laws of hospitality.

This is the first recorded instance of mob violence against
Jemima Wilkinson in six years of traveling and preaching.

Philadelphians made amends, however, in the attention
given the Universal Friend in the next few days. A day
or two after the mob attack she was given permission
to hold meetings in the Methodist Meeting House, a
spacious brick church still standing on Fourth Street
between Vine and Race and now called St. George's. It

may have been here that the Marquis de Chastellux, who
had first heard of her in Rhode Island, was unable to
get in to hear her. He noted, "I made an attempt to
hear her in Philadelphia in October, 1782, but the crowd
was so great, and, what is very uncommon in America,
so turbulent, that it was impossible to get near the place
of worship." A person who did get inside reported: "The
female preacher, after having sat some time in silence,
arose, and with an agreeable sweetness and elegance, with
propriety addressed the auditory, above one hours, and
that in such an awful and powerful manner, declaring
the truths of the gospel of Jesus Christ, that numbers
were convicted and bowed down under the power of
her ministry: and sighs and tears shed in abundance,
many confessing that such preaching and praying (for she
concluded with prayer) they had never been acquainted
with."[1]

The Marquis de Barbé-Marbois had better luck than
Chastellux in attending one of the meetings. He went
out of curiosity, with seven or eight French officers, and
was able to obtain a seat fairly near the pulpit. He
observed:

In spite of their being quite a number of us, and in spite of
the commotion which our unforseen arrival occasioned in the
assembly, she did not seem to see us, for she continued to
speak with ease and facility, her eyes lowered.

Her discourse seemed to us to be composed of commonplaces about the Bible and the Fathers. She enunciated so clearly, though without elegance, that I think she was reciting a
prepared sermon, and it was difficult for me to believe that
she was speaking from inspiration, or as the wordly say, extemporaneously. But, glancing at us Frenchmen, she seemed
to notice us for the first time. As she spoke of the attachment

people have for the things of this world, she continued thus:

"Amongst those who listen to me, how few have been led here by a desire for their salvation! Curiosity attracts them, they wish to be able to tell of extraordinary things when they return to their own country." I swear to you that at this moment I thought her a seer or a prophetess, and I expected to hear her mention my journal.

"Do these strangers believe that their presence in the house of the Lord flatters me? I disdain their honors, I scorn greatness and good fortune. Do not seek me, do not listen to me, unless you are touched by grace. Go away, no longer profane this temple, if you are still in the snares of the infernal angel. But if you are disposed to enter into the way of salvation, if my discourses have softened your hearts, if I can snatch a single one of you from the danger which he runs, I have not traveled too long a road in seeking it."

She was so moved, talking thus, that she was obliged to stop, and took out her handkerchief to dry her tears. We were surprised at the apostrophe, but perhaps as hardened as before.

Barbé-Marbois was favorably impressed after hearing her and wrote: "She lives soberly, her conduct is good, and her morals are irreproachable. . . . You can be sure that if she does not accomplish very much good, at any rate the perfect tolerance which they show her will do no harm." Chastellux, who did not meet her, was only able to repeat some of the stories about her that were circulating. She believed, or pretended to believe, he reported, that she was "the saviour of the world revived." Chastellux did meet the two young men, Arnold Potter and William Turpin, who came to his boarding house seeking lodgings, and described them as "tall, handsome young men . . . with large round flapped hats, and long flowing strait locks, with a sort of melancholy wildness in their countenances, and an effeminate dejected air." He complained that they would not enter into conversation with him.

Among those in the "prodigious crowds" attracted by the preaching of Jemima Wilkinson was the widower Christopher Marshall. Marshall was a retired druggist and paint merchant, a birthright member of the Society of Friends who was disowned for his sympathy with the cause of American independence. He was attracted to Jemima Wilkinson from the first and befriended her and her followers whenever they visited Philadelphia. Although he was never a follower of hers, he seemed to respect her mission and wrote her long letters discussing his religious views and explaining his differences of opinion. Jemima Wilkinson, Alice Hazard, and Sarah Brown were guests at his home on the night of October 6, 1782, and on October 10 the three women spent the night at the home of his daughter Sally, while William Potter and Thomas Hathaway stayed with his son Charles, and Arnold Potter and William Turpin stayed with his son Christopher, Jr. "I hope that this Visitation from Heaven will not be soon forgotten by many who seemed not to be reached with it," Christopher Marshall noted in his diary.

Another person who became one of the Universal Friend's first converts in Philadelphia was Jehu Eldridge, received into the Philadelphia Society of Friends in 1764 by certificate from the Haddonfield, New Jersey, Monthly Meeting. He began to speak at Jemima Wilkinson's meetings in October, 1782; in January, 1783, he was dismissed from unity with the Quakers.

Jemima Wilkinson's success in Philadelphia attracted the attention of Abraham Supplee, minister of the Bethel Methodist Church in Worcester, Pennsylvania, about eighteen miles from Philadelphia. He invited her to visit his home in Worcester and to preach in the Bethel Church, built in 1770 by his father as a nondenominational chapel. Abraham Supplee and the Universal Friend soon had a falling-out, but she was invited then to the home of his brother-in-law, David Wagener. The visit was a memorable date in the life of Wagener, who recorded:

1782, October ye 19. Came ye New England Friends to my House first, the same evening a meeting; next morning on ye first day of the week had a Great and powerful meeting to the communing and embellishing of my Soul—the same at my house again next day or second day, again at Bethel; meeting rather more powerful than the Day before, at the Same Meeting house. that day afternoon they took their leave from us and I and my father conducted them to Chris Funk that evening, lodged there that night, next day I went with them to Bethelem.

The Publick Friends' Names (the Universal Friend) or by name Chimima Wilkenson, Thomas Hathaway, Alice Hasard, William Potter, Arnold Potter, Sarah Brown, William Furniss [Turpin], all of New England, and Jehue Eldridge public friend from Philadelphia.

In the short time she spent in Philadelphia and vicinity on her first visit in 1782, Jemima Wilkinson attracted enough of a following to convince her that another visit was necessary. Jehu Eldridge was an avowed follower, and David Wagener was a likely prospect, as were many others in Philadelphia itself. The country girl from Cumberland, Rhode Island, had made her mark in the big city. Elizabeth Drinker, orthodox Quaker and Tory sympathizer, recorded in her diary: "Somedays past Jemima Wilkingson left this Town, a woman lately from New-England who has occasiond much talk in this City—she and those that accompany'd her, (who were call'd her Desciples) resided some short time in Elfrith's-Ally, where crowds went to hear her preach and afterwards in ye Methodast meeting-House—her Dress and Behavour, remarkable—"

Nearly two years passed before she returned a second time to Pennsylvania. Arnold Potter and Sarah Brown were her companions again, joined on this journey by Elizabeth Holmes of Stonington and Abraham Dayton of New Milford. This time the Universal Friend and her companions had friends in Philadelphia and the party of five found a welcome on August 13, 1784, at the home of Christopher Marshall, Jr. On this visit, the Free Quaker Meeting House, a new, sturdy brick building on the corner of Fifth and Arch streets, was made available to her, and again her meetings were crowded. Christopher Marshall estimated that three or four hundred attended her meeting on August 15, and six or seven hundred crowded in to hear her on August 17. The Free Quakers, sometimes called the "Fighting Quakers," were persons who had been disowned by the Society of Friends for participating, to various degrees, in the struggle for independence. Declaring that a defensive war was not sinful and rejecting the doctrine of nonresistance, they built their own meetinghouse in 1783. Marshall was active in their society, and undoubtedly his friendship for Jemima helped to secure the use of the meetinghouse for her. Probably the hospitality of the Free Quakers was influenced by the number of Wilkinson followers who sympathized with the Revolution and perhaps even by the attitude of Jemima herself, although she was careful never to express herself in public on any political question, including independence.

Jemima Wilkinson's presence in Philadelphia again attracted considerable attention. Jacob Hiltzheimer noticed a crowd around the Free Quaker Meeting House on August 15 and waited to watch Jemima Wilkinson come out, get into a chair, and drive away. He went to hear her preach at the meetinghouse on August 20 and observed that "she looks more like a man than a woman." In addition to her public appearances at the meetinghouse, she and her group held meetings in several private homes during her two weeks in Philadelphia. Christopher Marshall often had tea with the Universal Friend and either talked with her or attended one of her meetings every day she was in Philadelphia. "She seemed Sweet & lively in Conversation," he recorded in his diary. On August 28 she left Philadelphia to go to David Wagener's home in Worcester. From here she made a tour of New Jersey and returned to Philadelphia for another week in October, 1784. On October 14 she began her trip back to New England from Worcester, leaving behind the nucleus of a group of loyal followers.

A month after Jemima Wilkinson left the Philadelphia area to return to New England, an advertisement in the *Freeman's Journal* of November 24, 1784, announced: "Just Published, and to be Sold by Francis Bailey, *The Universal Friend's Advice*. Price six-pence." The item advertised was an eight-page pamphlet entitled *The Uni-*

versal Friend's Advice to Those of the Same Religious Society, Recommended to Be Read in Their Public Meetings for Divine Worship. This is the only printed work associated with Jemima Wilkinson other than the ill-fated plagiarism, *Some Considerations,* printed for her in Providence by Abner Brownell in 1779. *The Universal Friend's Advice* was evidently intended to be both a directive for the worship services of the society of Universal Friends and a statement of their religious beliefs. Arrangements for its printing were made by Christopher Marshall. He sent copies to Jemima Wilkinson by Thomas Hathaway, who had called on him on February 26, 1785, before returning to New England. Marshall recorded, "I gave him a number of the universal Friends advice that I had got printed for him to take home with him requesting him kindly to remember me to her, and to all her Friends that has any knowledge of me."

The Universal Friend's Advice seems to have no marked organization and consists almost entirely of quotations from the Bible or paraphrases of scriptural passages. In this respect it resembled the language of Jemima Wilkinson's letters and the descriptions of her ordinary speech. The instructions are simple and contain nothing original or unusual. "The Public Universal Friend Adviseth all, who desire to be *one* with the *friend* in spirit, and to be wise unto salvation," began the *Advice.* Universal Friends were enjoined to be punctual in attending meetings, to meet at the tenth hour of the day if possible or to sit in their homes at the time of meeting "to wait for and upon the Lord," and "to shun the company and conversation of the wicked *world.*"

Twice the injunction of the Golden Rule was repeated,

and in three different places worshipers were warned not to speak in meeting without being moved by the Holy Spirit. Members of the society were urged to use plainness of speech and apparel and to "live as you would be willing to die." The Universal Friend rephrased Christ's words (John 15:14), "Ye are my friends, if ye do whatsoever I command you," in the negative, "Ye cannot be my friends, except ye do whatsoever I command you." No mention was made about marriage or celibacy, although Paul's advice in Galatians 6:7-8 and Romans 8:6-18 was quoted. This small pamphlet, vague as it was, was the only published directive of the society of Universal Friends, and, as such, was reprinted twice after her death. During her lifetime, however, Jemima Wilkinson governed her society in person, or through trusted associates.[2]

Since the main body of her followers was in New England, Jemima Wilkinson spent most of her time there, but she did not neglect her new friends in Philadelphia and Worcester. Members of her society were sent to Pennsylvania to keep alive the interest stimulated by the Universal Friend on her successful second visit. Thomas Hathaway arrived in Philadelphia by boat from Dartmouth, Massachusetts, in September, 1784, and spent the winter there. In the fall of 1785, James Parker was sent to Pennsylvania on a preaching tour. David Wagener introduced him in Philadelphia, but at the Free Quaker Meeting House, where Jemima Wilkinson herself had attracted such crowds the year before, Parker was interrupted and forbidden to speak. Parker evidently won no new support for the Universal Friends. He wrote to Christopher Marshall, signing his letter, "Known by the

name of James Parker." Such pretensions did not impress
Philadelphians; a devastating description of him was
printed in *The Freeman's Journal* in 1787.

James Parker . . . appears to be about 45 years of age, is
artful, conceited, and illiterate; and as the countenance of a
man is sometimes a tell tale, so those who are skilled in physiog-
nomy, may see in his face the cunning which lies hid in his
heart, though varnished over with an apparent candour and
freedom in conversation: and as he possesses none of the fire
of a divine enthusiast, so neither does he possess that zeal
which is necessary to complete the character of an imposter;
he is crafty, but cold and unanimating, and that moderate
share of understanding which he possesses, does not appear
so much clouded with an imagination of his own sanctity, as
he appears desirous of making others believe him a saint; and
on the whole, it seems as if he endeavoured to be great among
this mistaken people, from a principle of a most ridiculous
kind of vanity, and for the sake of an indolent life.

After Parker's failure to exercise effective leadership of
the Pennsylvania Universal Friends, Sarah Richards was
sent to Worchester in November, 1786, to take charge
of the group in that vicinity. She was welcomed at the
home of David Wagener, who had committed himself to
the Universal Friend's society.

David Wagener grew up in the Schwenkfelder faith of
his parents, but later joined the Methodists and married
Rebecca Supplee, whose brother was a Methodist minister.
Wagener continued to be dissatisfied, however, and was
turning toward the Quakers, whom he thought to be
"nearest to the Scripture truths," when he met Jemima
Wilkinson. He was immediately impressed and declared,
"When I heard the Gospel's Trump sound, I knew it was
the true sound, and that it was with great power from

on high, even to the convincing and converting of souls that heard and obeyed the counsel delivered." After the Universal Friend's second visit to Pennsylvania in 1784, he joined her society, and from then on furnished hospitality for the Universal Friends who came to Worcester. Wagener had inherited one farm in Worcester from his father and had purchased another from the Supplees. He and his sister Anna became important sources of material support for the Universal Friend.

David Wagener's home was the scene of an incident on January 4, 1787, that brought Jemima Wilkinson much unpleasant publicity, even though she was in Rhode Island at the time. The Wagener house was filled with members of the Universal Friend's society and other guests who joined in religious services under the leadership of Sarah Richards. From New England had come Abigail Dayton, wife of Abraham Dayton of New Milford. Also present were Anna Steyers, a friend of the Wageners, and, from Philadelphia, Rachel Malin, Mary Bramall, and Mary's sister Sarah Wilson. During the religious meeting, Sarah Wilson and Abigail Dayton had a disagreement, and later that evening Sarah became convinced that Abigail tried to strangle her while she slept. Sarah left the Wagener house much upset, and nearly three months later, on March 28, 1787, a long and detailed account of her alleged experiences was published in a Philadelphia newspaper. The essence of her story was that Abigail Dayton, in trying to murder her, had, by mistake, choked her bedmate, Anna Steyers. A reply from Abigail, who had returned to New Milford, was published on August 22, giving her side of the incident, and, on September 5, a rejoinder by Sarah Wilson appeared.

The members of the society who were present in the

house at the time attributed Sarah Wilson's fears to a bad dream or nightmare, and Anna Steyers, who was supposed to be the person choked, denied any knowledge of such an incident. When Jemima Wilkinson again came to Philadelphia, on May 20, 1788, she met Sarah, or Sally, Wilson at a meeting in a private home. According to Christopher Marshall, Sarah acknowledged that she had been persuaded to publish her story, which was exaggerated in the publication. She still insisted, however, that she could not "get shut of the fears she was struck with at David Waggoners." Marshall reported, however, that "they appeared to be reconcilled shaked hands and in love partest." The Wilson charges, based on the hallucinations of an emotional woman and exaggerated in the press, were widely reprinted and used to discredit the Universal Friend. Eventually the episode passed into folklore and was told as a story in which Jemima herself tried to strangle Sarah Wilson.

In addition to the furor over Sarah Wilson, the Universal Friend and her followers received other attention in the Philadelphia press. On February 14, 1787, Jemima Wilkinson was attacked in an anonymous article in both *The Freeman's Journal* and *The American Museum*, which was subsequently reprinted in other publications. It began:

The religious imposture, which is intended to be exposed in this essay, is too ridiculous in itself to merit a moment's attention, were it not, that some virtuous people are, and some may yet be drawn into the snare, and by degrees at length involved in the most fatal labyrinth of error.

A defense of Jemima Wilkinson and her followers, dated February 23, was published in *The American Museum*, but not in *The Freeman's Journal*. Then on March 28,

1787, the whole front page and half of page two of *The Freeman's Journal* was devoted to a long answer to the defense and a continued attack on the Universal Friend. The brunt of all of this unfavorable publicity fell upon Sarah Richards, who was in Worcester, although it also disturbed Jemima Wilkinson in New England when she learned of the developments.

In a letter to Sarah Richards, dated the eleventh of the third month, 1787, from South Kingstown, she expressed her opinion of Philadelphians in strong Biblical prose.

Dear Blessed Soul . . . I have Been verry much troubled about thee for fear of Treacherous Dealers Under the pretence of being friends to thee, I have been to Philadelphia more than once, and am Some acquainted with people there, with their ways & their Doings — And due Know if it ware possible they would Deceive the verry Elect . . .

I believe that the wicked will find some other Business to due before it is long Besides publishing me and them that Desire to due well in News Papers, Dont be troubled Dear Soul. . . . Altho the Seas Roar and fullness thereof yet the Lord on high is mightyer than the Noise of many waters, ye than the Mighty waves of the Sea. His Testamonys are verry Sure, And Blessed are they that due his Commandments that they may have a Right to the tree of Life, and may Enter in through the Gates into the Holy City. But the fearfull and Unbelieving & abominable & Dogs, & sorcerers and Whoremungers and all Lyers shall have their part in the Lake that Burns with fire & Brimstone—

By the end of 1787 Jemima Wilkinson and her society had completed the plans to establish a New Jerusalem, and most of her New England followers were prepared to leave whenever the location should be determined. The time seemed appropriate for a third visit to Pennsylvania to consult with the members of the society there. This time the Universal Friend traveled the shore route from Rhode Island through Stonington, Groton, New London, Killingsworth, Guilford, New Haven (where she held a meeting on the Court House steps), Milford, Stratford, Fairfield, Norwalk, Stamford, and to New York City. Crossing the river, she passed through Elizabethtown, Woodbridge, and Princeton, went around Philadelphia, directly to the Wagener stone farmhouse in Worcester, where she arrived on December 1, 1787.

One of David Wagener's houses, the old Supplee place, built in 1733, was placed at her disposal. This farm included the northern slope and summit of Methacton Hill and, near the house, a small stream that ran into Zacharia Creek. The top of the hill afforded a sweeping view of the Perkiomen valley toward the west and the Schuylkill valley toward the east. From this location Washington had been able to watch the British moving into Philadelphia in 1777, and near here the Continental Army had camped along the Skippack Pike on their way to, and in retreat from, the battle of Germantown. Another Rhode Islander, Nathaniel Green, had made his headquarters in a small stone building attached to the house, and in the field southeast of the house General Green had met with Washington for a conference before the battle of Germantown. This was rich, fertile farming country, and Wagener and other of the Pennsylvania followers were more reluctant to leave it for the wilderness than the New Englanders were to quit their stony acres.

Not until May, 1788, did the Universal Friend come into Philadelphia. The adverse newspaper publicity had stirred up so much opposition that, wherever she held meetings, noisy crowds gathered in the street around the house or meeting place. In spite of this she preached to a large congregation at the Presbyterian meetinghouse on Arch Street. One of her sermons was described in some detail by Christopher Marshall:

Her discourse was grave, manly, and reverent, recomending with degree of power a state of repentence. "The way to attain was in the first place ceasing to evil. Secondly the total renouncing of the spirit of this world, and casting ourselves thro faith into the arms of Jesus Christ, the Son of God who came, dwelt, and suffered in the flesh for our redemption, and that all who laid hold of this proffered salvation Should be saved of the Lord. on the reverse destruction must be the consequences and these states we should all witness when we were all disembodied from this earthly tabernacle."

Marshall met and visited with Jemima Wilkinson nearly every day she was in Philadelphia, and he wrote about her respectfully in his diary. Although they spoke frankly on religious matters, even Marshall found it difficult to get information on some subjects. On August 18, 1784, he was in conversation with her before a meeting, having "some considerable discourse with Jemimah respecting Dress": "I think she did not wish I should proceed, as I gave her to understand that has she had caused to speak I should be free & open she laid her hand on her mouth. So I stopt not willing to ofend." Sometimes Marshall showed annoyance at those who criticized the Universal Friend out of ignorance. On May 3, 1788, the day Jemima left Philadelphia to return to Worcester, Marshall

talked with Joseph Warner's wife, who, he noted, had a
great "deal to say to the prejudice of Jemima, yet she
knows nothing but hear say or reading Newspapers."
Marshall's own credo was expressed in a letter he wrote
to his friend Peter Miller, head of the Ephrata Community, in 1774.

> I take kindly thy sentiment respecting of my house being
> still as an assylum for all indegent castoff. . . . I could wish
> that I could make it so, notwithstanding the ill treatment, by ap-
> probious language I have met with on that account. Yet never-
> theless I hope that no discouragements in that way, will have
> force enough to prevent me. But on the other hand, that both
> my Heart & House I pray be kept wide open, for the recep-
> tion and comfort of all those, whom the self righeouse Bigot,
> Scribe, and Pharisees of our age, may reject, banish, and con-
> temn, as unworthy of (their Heaven) their notice and regard.

The many similarities between the society of Universal
Friends and Ephrata Community suggest that the older
community may have influenced Jemima Wilkinson. If
so, Christopher Marshall would be the logical link. Not
only had Marshall visited Ephrata while he lived at Lan-
caster during the British occupation of Philadelphia but
he corrected the English manuscript of the history of the
community in 1777. It would be surprising if he had
not talked with Jemima about his friend Peter Miller and
the society at Ephrata in his religious discussions with
her. Certainly the similarity in the beliefs and practices
of the two sects is striking. The Universal Friends, like
Ephrata Community, had no written covenant, no creed
or confession of faith, and took no vows, basing their
religious beliefs on a literal interpretation of the Bible.
Their positions on celibacy were identical. Celibacy was

considered more virtuous, as Paul advised, but marriage was not prohibited and married couples were not required to separate in either society.

The German Baptists of Ephrata observed the sabbath on the seventh day. It is not clear when the Universal Friends adopted this practice, but it seems to be some time after Jemima Wilkinson's first visit to Pennsylvania in 1782. The example of Ephrata may have influenced her dream of a self-sufficient community of believers apart from the world, which became a plan of action after her first two visits to Philadelphia. In Jemima Wilkinson's Jerusalem, however, there was no common ownership of property, although some such idea seems to have been considered in the formative plans. Instead each member of the society owned his own land and worked as an individual, donating some of his time and substance for the support of the Universal Friend and her household. At Ephrata, property belonged to the community, and the labor of the celibate brethren and sisters was for the common fund, although none of the members were required to give up any of their possessions or to donate to the common fund; some individuals made voluntary contributions to support the ministry and to provide for the aged and poor of the society. Hospitality to those in need or distress and to all travelers was a tradition at Ephrata, whose buildings were used as a hospital for the sick and wounded of Washington's army during the Revolution. When the Universal Friend had a home of her own in Jerusalem, her doors, like those of Ephrata, were always open to the needy and to travelers. Like the Ephratans, Jemima Wilkinson believed that the use of arms and recourse to law were unchristian and unbecoming, although, like them, she too seemed to sympathize with the struggle for independence. Although the community that Jemima Wilkinson began to plan in the years 1785 and 1786 was similar in several respects to Ephrata, the Universal Friends did not adopt the Ephrata cloister's practices of baptism by immersion, observance of the Lord's Supper, or use of music or hymn singing in worship.

By the fall of 1788, Jemima Wilkinson had spent nearly a year in Pennsylvania. In that time the pioneer party had established the Friend's settlement in the Genesee country in western New York. Communications with the new settlement, such as they were, were better from Worcester than from New England. Some families needed the personal encouragement of the Universal Friend before giving up their familiar homes to move to the frontier. Decisions had to be made about the property owned by the society, meetinghouses in East Greenwich and New Milford and one under construction in Smithfield, Rhode Island. This last trip to New England was a short one. Jemima left Worcester in November, 1788, and returned in February, 1789. She did not visit Philadelphia during her final year at Worcester. All her energy and her thoughts were devoted to the plans for her New Jerusalem in the wilderness, which she set out to join in March, 1790.

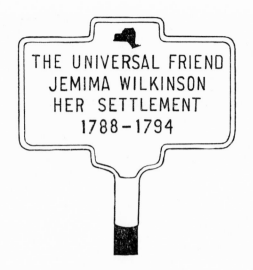

THE UNIVERSAL FRIEND
JEMIMA WILKINSON
HER SETTLEMENT
1788-1794

Chapter VI

Wilderness Sanctuary

HAD Jemima Wilkinson sought only personal comfort and material advantages, she could have remained in the "Old Abbey" in Little Rest or the comfortable stone farmhouse in Worcester. Instead, she rejected the conveniences of settled society, and turning to the wilderness, accepted the crude life of a frontier pioneer in order to gather about her a community of the faithful. "I have long prayed that there might be a peaceable habitation for me & my friends to dwell somewhere," she wrote James Parker in 1788. "Now if you have found a good Countery where you can live together & desire me to come & dwell with you I must tell you on what conditions I am willing to come &

no other." These conditions, recorded after the first party of pioneers had actually broken ground at the new settlement, described the type of community the Universal Friend wished to see established. "If there could be a sufficient tract of Land procur'd & purchased for friends & a township laid out where none but friends hold any title or profession there I should be willing to dwell what few remaining days I may spend here in time . . . [but] let them know I am determined not to dwell with revilers for I am weary of them that hate peace."

At the beginning of her ministry the Publick Universal Friend traveled widely, declaring that her mission was to preach to the unregenerate world. From the very beginning, however, it was clear that she was not seeking martyrdom, despite such frequent exclamations as "My earthly house of this tabernacle must be dissolved," and "I shall soon be called to lay aside this mortal body, and stand disembodied before the Lord." She avoided areas where strong opposition developed and suffered none of the physical violence that Mother Ann Lee met in western and central Massachusetts. When noisy, unruly crowds threatened her in Philadelphia, she shook the dust of the city from her feet and retired to more hospitable Worcester. By 1784, when *The Universal Friend's Advice* was published, she evidently despaired of saving the whole world and sought only to bring together her scattered congregation. "Shun the company and conversation of the wicked world," she warned as she began to make plans for a community away from the corroding influences of contemporary society.

Jemima Wilkinson may have been influenced by the success of the Shaker community at Niskayuna, New York, or the example of the well-established Ephrata Community in Pennsylvania. Whatever her source of inspiration, the idea of establishing a community of Universal Friends was brought up after her return to New England from Pennsylvania in 1784. It was natural that the discussion about a site for such a colony should turn to the Genesee country. This homeland of the Seneca Indians was virtually unknown to the whites until after General John Sullivan's expedition in 1779. General John Sullivan—the same who gave Jemima Wilkinson permission to go to England in 1778—was commissioned to punish the Iroquois for their support of the British. He and his men returned from western New York full of enthusiastic stories about the rich fertile land, the fine lakes and clear streams, and hardwood forests full of game. The men who had seen this country and those with whom they talked burned to exploit the wealth of this new land, sparsely populated by the defeated Indians.

The Genesee country was also coveted in British Canada. Here Loyalists who had fought for the British cause and, in defeat, were unable to return to their homes saw an opportunity to recoup their fortunes with the aid of their former Iroquois allies. British influence in the region disseminated from garrisons on American soil at Fort Niagara and Fort Oswego, both held in defiance of the terms of the peace treaty of 1783. But British intrigue and Indian title to the land were not the only complications that faced potential settlers in the Genesee country. In addition, the whole region was the subject of a dispute by New York and Massachusetts, each citing their colonial charters to support conflicting claims.

Not until December, 1786, did representatives of the two states, meeting in Hartford, work out a compromise agreement. Massachusetts recognized the right of New

York to governmental jurisdiction over the whole territory
in dispute and, in return, New York ceded to Massachusetts title to the land in the western part of the state. Massachusetts thus received the pre-emption right, or right of
first purchase subject to Indian titles, of the land west of a
line to run due north from the eighty-second milestone on
the Pennsylvania boundary line. The actual survey of this
so-called Pre-emption Line was not made until the summer of 1788, however.

This remote, rich territory naturally attracted the attention of Jemima Wilkinson and her followers as they
sought a location for their community. Scouts were sent
out to explore the country in 1785. Jeptha Wilkinson,
Jemima's younger brother, went directly from Rhode Island to the Genesee country and spent the winter there,
living with the Indians and exploring and mapping the
region, using Indian guides. Jeptha returned to New England with an enthusiastic report that especially interested
William Potter and his son Arnold. Another Rhode Islander, Ezekial Shearman, also explored the country in the early
spring of 1786. He followed the route of Sullivan's army,
up the Susquehanna River from Pennsylvania. Shearman
was more pessimistic. It was March when he reached the
lake country, with two Indian traders as guides, yet it
took them five days to wade through the deep snow from
Newtown Flats (Elmira) to Kanadesaga (Geneva). The
destruction of the Indian villages by Sullivan's forces impressed Shearman, who felt that the hostility of the Indians
because of their sufferings made it "too soon to enter the
sad, dark, land of the lakes."

Neither Shearman's cautious report nor the confusion
over the title to the region discouraged the Universal
Friends. At a meeting of the principal members of the

society at New Milford, Connecticut, in 1786, the decision was made to locate their settlement in the Genesee country. A committee of three, including Thomas Hathaway, Sr., Abraham Dayton, and Richard Smith, was sent to explore the region and to recommend a site for the colony. The exploring party set out in 1787, going first to Philadelphia and following the trail of Sullivan's march through central Pennsylvania. In the Wyoming Valley they heard glowing accounts of the region around Seneca Lake and continued along Sullivan's route to Kanadesaga and down the west side of the lake to Kashong. Here they were entertained by two French traders who confirmed their own favorable impression of the country. They did not attempt to fix the exact site of the settlement, leaving that for the advance party, but they did resolve that it should be in the vicinity of Seneca Lake.

Another member of the Universal Friend's society explored the Genesee country later that same year. Benjamin Brown, Jr., came alone and proceeded farther west to the vicinity of Big Tree (Geneseo). The winter snows caught him there, and he was forced to remain encamped with the Indians until March, 1788. Here he became acquainted with Mary Jemison, the famous White Woman of the Genesee, who lived as the wife of a Seneca chief, with her large family, by the Genesee River. Whatever Brown reported after his return to New England, however, had no effect on the decision to establish the settlement near Seneca Lake. The first party of pioneers set out for the new country later in the spring after he returned.

At the New Milford meeting of 1786 a fund had been established to purchase the land for the new settlement. No document remains to reveal the exact nature of the compact that was formed, and an investigator, seeking in-

formation only fifty years after the death of the Universal
Friend, found that stories on the subject were not clear
even then. There is no indication that a true community
of property was ever planned. Although the land was to
be purchased in one piece for the whole community of
Universal Friends, it was not to be owned in common, and
the fund that was set up was not a true common purse.
Each member of the society who contributed was given a
receipt and expected to receive title to a piece of land
proportionate to his investment. Not all those who wished
to emigrate had the means to pay their way, however. As
James Parker explained in a petition to Governor Clinton
and the Commissioners of the Land Office, "Several familys
among us we have helped there, & Intended to helped them
to Some Lands because they could not help them Selves.
Some other familys put in a little Money & when they got
there Expected a little Land, where they Expected to
raise Support for them Selves & familys." Evidently it was
believed that land in the new country would be plentiful
and cheap enough so that any member of the society who
wished to participate in the settlement would be helped
by the group to secure enough land to support himself
and his family even if he could not contribute a proportionate share in the purchase fund. James Parker was
authorized to collect the money and give receipts and to
negotiate the purchase of the land.

Parker soon ran into trouble which he described in his
petition:

Before we began this removal [to New York State] we
Sent Messengers to Explore in Several places. & finaly gave
the preference to the Geneseo Country. This was about the
time the Leasee Company was Executeing their plans And

they told us it would be a Great advantage to us to be Concerned with them. & no harm to any body, for altho it was not lawful to buy lands of the Indians without power from the State, Yet there was no law against hireing lands of the Indians. And theirs was a Lease & not a Deed of Sale. And they further said they had Council Learned in the Law associated with them, and they had also Consulted with Council Learned in the Law for a fee and both ware of opinion it was no breach of Law their so taking a lease of the Indians. And we being Strangers in the State they took us in (Not in the Scripture Sense) but for about £800 of New York Currancy.

Poor Parker was "taken in" indeed, and the eight hundred pounds included not only some of his own money but that of the smaller investors of the society. A group of about eighty New York speculators, headed by John Livingston of "Livingston Manor," and Caleb Benton, had joined with a group of Canadian speculators, including the notorious Tory, Colonel John Butler, to organize the New York Genesee Land Company and the Niagara Genesee Land Company in 1787. The American company made its headquarters at Hudson, New York, and the Canadian at British-held Fort Niagara. Although the constitution of the state of New York forbade the purchase of Indian lands by private individuals, the backers of these companies thought they had discovered a loophole in the law. Using British and Tory influence, they obtained from the Indians a nine-hundred-and-ninety-nine-year *lease* to all of the lands of the Six Nations in the State of New York except for some small reservations. Thus they became known as the Lessee Company.

Recognizing that their title was somewhat tenuous, to say the least, the Lessees were ready to offer land in the

Genesee country at bargain rates. In Parker they found an eager bargain hunter. Enthusiastically he wrote to Abraham Dayton in New Milford from the Lessee headquarters in Hudson, New York, on April 14, 1788, that he had secured six townships, six miles square "as good Title as to any land in the world and the best land I ever seen in this world." He declared with pride, "It appears that my ventures and Labours has saved 40. or 50. or 60. or near a hundred Thousand Dollars for Friends." Parkers' rejoicing was short-lived. Governor George Clinton of New York denounced the Lessee maneuver and warned the Indians that they were the victims of a fraud. The legislature then passed an act that declared the Lessee title null and void. A subdued Parker wrote, "But when we heard that the Legislature of the State Disapproved of the Leasee Company proceedings we agreed with Oliver Phelps for some land, and went into that Country to begin our Settlement in the Spring of the year 1788."

Oliver Phelps and Nathaniel Gorham headed a group of New England land speculators who were successful in purchasing all of the lands west of the Pre-emption Line awarded to Massachusetts in the agreement with New York in 1786. They failed to get the approval of the legislature in 1787, but in 1788 they were able to buy the rights of the state to about six million acres of land for one million dollars in the depreciated currency of Massachusetts. Oliver Phelps conducted most of the business for the Phelps and Gorham associates. But when he came to western New York to extinguish the Indian title to the land, he found the influence of the Lessee group so strong with the Iroquois that he gave the Lessee Company four townships as a settlement for a sum paid toward twenty shares in the Phelps-Gorham purchase and to quiet its opposition to his negotiations with the Indians. In a treaty at Buffalo Creek in July, 1788, Phelps was successful in securing the title to two and a half million acres of land from the Pre-emption Line to west of the Genesee River, the Indians agreeing to retire west of the Phelps-Gorham purchase.

Out of the grant that Phelps made to the Lessee Company, James Parker and his associates in the society of Universal Friends received from Caleb Benton on November 28, 1788, the title to 1,104 acres in a strip six miles long and ninety-two rods wide that came to be known as the Garter. This was all that the society received for its eight hundred pounds, paid to the New York Genesee Company for the three and a quarter shares purchased by Parker. Parker's unhappy bargain-hunting wiped out most of the capital of the smaller investors in the society and shattered the plans to help the poorer members of the society locate in the new settlement. Jonathan Botsford, who advanced money to Parker, expecting to receive one thousand acres of land, complained that his share from the Lessee Company grant came to only thirteen or fourteen acres.

In the meantime the pioneer party of Universal Friends had already reached the Genesee country in the spring of 1788. Twenty-five persons, most of whom were New Englanders, made up this advance party under the leadership of James Parker.[1] Legend has it that the group was camped on the east side of Seneca Lake when they heard the sound of falling water across the lake and, traveling around, found a waterfall on the Outlet of Crooked (now Keuka) Lake. With such an excellent mill site available, it was decided to settle in that vicinity. The spot selected was a knoll, optimistically named City Hill, about a mile south of the Outlet and a mile back from the lake. Parker reported that they waited a "Considerable time at great Expense before Phelpses Treaty with the Indians was Compleated."

And when that treaty was over the Ceason was so far Spent that if we had waited to have the preemption line run before we began Improvement we Must a lost our Crops for that year which would a hurt us greatly, And by the best Information we could then get Concerning the preemption line we Expected in would run across Senaca Lake somewhere, therefore we Settled where we now are Expecting it was on our own Lands which we obtained by Contract with Oliver Phelps.

The survey of the first Pre-emption Line began in July and was not completed until late August or early September, 1788. Had it run due north from the eighty-second milestone on the Pennsylvania line as it was supposed to, the line would have passed through Seneca Lake, and both the Friend's Settlement and the village of Geneva would have been west of the line in the Phelps-Gorham purchase. Instead the line was twisted in an erratic but decidedly westerly direction that left most of the improvements of the Friend's Settlement as well as Geneva to the east of the line and outside the Phelps-Gorham tract. Making all due allowances for the inaccuracy of the survey instruments, the conclusion is inescapable that fraud was involved in the placement of the line and that members of the Lessee Company who wished to keep the strategic location of Geneva, at the foot of Seneca Lake, out of the hands of Phelps and Gorham were implicated. Oliver Phelps gave up his plan to make Geneva his headquarters and opened his land office at Canandaigua, twenty miles west, at the northern end of Canandaigua Lake. More seriously inconvenienced, however, were the settlers at the Friend's Settlement, who found they had invested backbreaking labor and made improvements on land to which they had no title.

Making a home in the wilderness required brutal, crushing work that even religious zeal could not mitigate. There were some clearings in the Genesee country where the Indians had raised corn and squash and even the remains of Indian orchards with a few apples hanging on shoots that grew up from the stumps left by Sullivan's army. But the site selected by the Universal Friends was virgin land, heavily wooded with beech, sugar maple, basswood, hickory, walnut, oak, and other trees. The trees were first cut and burned for the potash, and wheat was sown without plowing, using a harrow to break the soil. The pioneer party of twenty-five managed to get twelve acres cleared and planted to wheat in that first summer. They lived in tents at first and later in rude log houses. Game was plentiful; the country was full of deer. Bears and wolves were common, although they were not so great a nuisance as later, when pigs and sheep were introduced by the settlers. The greatest inconveniences in getting the land cleared were rattlesnakes, insects, and malaria, or "Genesee Fever." James Parker, the group's leader, became ill early in the summer, and Sarah Richards was sent from Pennsylvania to nurse him.

Jemima Wilkinson spent the winter of 1787-1788 and the following summer in Worcester, but she kept in touch with the development of the settlement. Sarah Richards returned before September and gave her "a good account of that new Country," but, evidently, a rather critical analysis of some of the settlers. Parker also had some unflattering comments to make about his fellow pioneers, who seem to have resented his exercise of authority. He wrote a report to the Universal Friend on September 17, 1788:

> Thos. Hathaway went home before frd. Potter came Tender & meaning to due well. He went in Company with the following Persons—John Briggs week and darkened tho Intending well. Young Peleg Briggs often the [?]   Young Thomas Shannon [Sherman], a poor Odd Creature. Gideon Aldrich Not much better off. Stephen Card in actual & open Rebellion (I think) John Reynolds very near that, tho Some drop of hope of him. Sheffield Luther was nothing & remains so. Augustus Barber is as he was. . . . I am sorry to have it to say Benjᵃ. Brown is Greatly hurt & burying his good Desires too much where the Slothful Servt. Bury'd his Talent. many complaints come against him. I fear from too Solid a Foundation. I think I can Say I rejoice in hope there will be a day of Judgement. O! the gripeing & Grinding Worldly-mindedness. with Pittyful Shifts of low Policy, with other Deviltry that I hear of is almost too much to think off—War it not for the Friends Sake & for the sake of a few others, I should be willing to flee many miles further into the Wilderness. Nevertheless not my will but thine be done.

In December, 1788, the Universal Friend returned to Rhode Island. Soon after she arrived in Little Rest, Arnold Potter came back from the Genesee country, where he had located two townships west of the settlement made by Parker. Acting for himself and his father, Judge William Potter, he purchased the land from Phelps and Gorham, but reported that Parker was still with the Lessees and that their company was in difficulty. Evidently the Universal Friend continued to support Parker as leader of the small colony. While most of the first group returned to New England for the winter of 1788-1789, Parker and a few others wintered over in the new settlement. The rugged New York winter under such primitive conditions was hard indeed. On the eighteenth of February, 1789, Elizabeth Holmes, wife of Jedidiah, was the first of the Universal Friends to "leave time" in the New Jerusalem. There were no boards for a coffin, so a log was hollowed out, the body sealed in with a slab, and Elizabeth Holmes became the first burial in City Hill Cemetery, in a grave hacked out of the frozen earth.

In February, 1789, the Universal Friend proceeded to Worcester and prepared to join the colony on the west side of Seneca Lake. Although Parker called the settlement "Jerusalem" in his letter in September, 1788, the most common name for this location in the early years was the Friend's Settlement. Later, after the second survey of the Pre-emption Line, it was usually known as the Gore. Conditions at the Friend's Settlement were still primitive, food was scarce, and hardship was commonplace when Jemima Wilkinson left Worcester in 1789 to join her people. About fifty miles from Worcester, Barnabus Brown, who was driving the coach carrying the Universal Friend and Mehitable Smith, attempted to ford flood-swollen Bushkill Creek. The waters were too high for the horses, who swam for safety; the occupants of the carriage were soaked and the Universal Friend almost drowned. The shock was so severe that she had to return to Worcester and did not attempt the trip again that year.

When the Universal Friend again set out for the settlement in western New York in the spring of 1790, conditions there were much improved. This time the journey was without incident. A number of the women close to Jemima Wilkinson, including Ruth Prichard, left Worcester in late February and went as far as Wyoming, Pennsylvania. There they remained, helping to pay for their lodgings by spinning and sewing, until March 18, when Jemima Wilkinson, Sarah Richards, and others joined them. The whole party, consisting of the Universal Friend, Sarah, twelve other members of the society of Universal Friends, and other passengers, left Wyoming on March 23 by boat. Up the Susquehanna the boat slowly made its way past Wyalusing, Standing Stone, Wysox, and Sheshequin to Tioga Point (Athens), Chemung, and Newtown (Elmira) on the Chemung River, fifteen exhausting days from Wyoming. Where a house was situated near the river, the boat stopped and the Universal Friend held a meeting. Sometimes she addressed a group of people on the riverbank and once rebuked a man who refused to sell the party potatoes on the sabbath by preaching, "He that regardedth the day, He regardedth unto the Lord; & he that regardedth not the day to the Lord, he doth not regard it."

The Universal Friend and Sarah Richards, who was sick most of the trip, usually slept in a carriage on board the boat. The rest of the party spent the nights in a tent on shore or crowded in to take shelter under the roof of a hospitable pioneer. Cold March rains and a bit of April snow added to the hardship of the journey. When at last the boat reached Newtown, the Universal Friend led a prayer of thanksgiving before the carriage was unloaded. From here the route was by land to the head of Seneca Lake. Those of the group who proceeded on foot actually made better time than Jemima Wilkinson and her carriage. They passed through Catherine's Town (Montour Falls) to David Culver's cabin on the site of present-day Watkins Glen. Here a group from the Friend's Settlement met the travelers from Pennsylvania, and the reunited Universal Friends had a "Great exhortation" on the evening of April 10. Three days later, on Tuesday, April 13, 1790, the Universal Friend and her followers set off by boat and completed the last twenty miles to the awaiting settlement before sunset. "The Friend had a Prayer by the Shoar," and that evening the whole settlement joined in a great meeting of rejoicing.

Some of the settlers had toiled on the frontier for two long years, and many of the others had not seen their spiritual leader since she had left New England more than a year before. They had much to show her. With two hundred and sixty people counted by the census takers of the new federal government in 1790, their settlement was the largest by far in western New York, more than two and a half times larger than either Geneva or Canadaigua. It was still a raw, frontier community, however. A road ran through stump-studded fields and patches of woods from the landing on the lake to Smith's Mills on the Outlet of Crooked Lake. Here, where the water fell some forty or forty-five feet, a gristmill and a sawmill were erected. The gristmill, which saved difficult trips to Tioga Point, was very important in the economy of the community. The stones were purchased by members of the society in New Milford before the fall of 1788, and were transported by bateaux to the landing and hauled on ox sleds to the mill site. Richard Smith, James Parker, and Abraham Dayton all owned shares in the mill, which was completed on the

Fourth of July, 1790. On July 5, Richard Smith wrote in his Bible with the care he would take to announce the birth of a new child, "I have this day ground ten bushels of wheat the same having been raised in the immediate neighborhood last year (1789)."

All the dwellings were log structures when Jemima Wilkinson first arrived. She and her companions were housed temporarily in a small cabin not far from a waterfall on a creek that ran into Seneca Lake a bit south of the Outlet. This cabin evidently belonged to Thomas Hathaway and was used only until a more suitable house for the Universal Friend could be built. The site for her house was a piece of high ground on the south side of the same creek, about a mile from the lake shore. This was indeed a spacious building by frontier standards. Reputed to be the first frame house in New York State west of Seneca Lake, it was built by Elijah Malin and paid for, in part at least, by Anna Wagener. Built around a central chimney with nine fireplaces, the house was two stories high with a gambrel roof. Originally the building was covered with hand-sawed, inch-and-a-half-thick planks nailed in place vertically with hand-wrought nails. Pictures of later date show that it was eventually covered with horizontal siding. Small though it seems, this dwelling housed the Universal Friend and her considerable entourage from 1790, when it was completed, until 1794, when she moved farther west.

Not far from the Universal Friend's home a log meetinghouse was constructed in the summer of 1790. This crude structure was about thirty feet square, with a preaching platform across the east end, and was heated by a fireplace. Not only were religious services held there,

Jemima as a young woman. This portrait is probably an artist's conception; it was copyrighted in 1873 by Stafford C. Cleveland. Reproduced by courtesy of the Yates County Historical Society.

The Universal Friend's first house in western New York. Built in 1790, it was her home until 1794, when she moved to Jerusalem. The building, shown in a photograph taken in 1890, no longer stands.

The second house in western New York, her first in Jerusalem. From Stafford C. Cleveland's *History and Directory of Yates County*.

but it was also used as a schoolhouse, and both Sarah Richards and Ruth Prichard taught classes there.

Jemima Wilkinson might have been well satisfied by the end of 1790. She was comfortably settled in the midst of nearly three hundred of her followers, and many others back in New England and Pennsylvania were ready to emigrate to the new Jerusalem. Much hard work remained to be done, but the prospects for a prosperous colony of believers looked good. Faraway events were taking place, however, that shattered the tranquillity of the small sect and destroyed Jemima Wilkinson's dream. The story is a complicated one and national politics played a role. When Alexander Hamilton, appointed Secretary of the Treasury of the new United States government in 1789, pushed through his measure to assume the state debts and to pay them at full face value, the depreciated currency of Massachusetts nearly doubled in value. The Phelps and Gorham associates, unable to raise the full amount to pay for their land purchase, surrendered about two thirds of their grant to the state of Massachusetts in return for a clear title to the remaining third, for which they had secured the Indian rights. This portion of about two million acres between the Pre-emption Line and the Genesee River they then sold to Robert Morris in November, 1790, excepting about fifty townships already disposed of. Even before this transaction was fully completed, Robert Morris, the "Financier of the Revolution," resold the whole tract at a substantial profit to a group of British speculators known as the Pulteney Associates. They sent a Scotsman, Charles Williamson, as their agent to supervise their investment. In less than six months the region chosen by the Universal Friends for their wilderness refuge had three different owners, and each change of hands drove land values higher and higher.

Another factor affecting the Friend's Settlement even more directly was the peregrinating Pre-emption Line. The first survey located the line to the west of most of the improvements made by the Universal Friends near Seneca Lake, indicating that their location belonged to New York State. To secure a valid title to the land, James Parker, on behalf of the society, spent three weeks in New York City in late April and early May of 1791, petitioning Governor George Clinton and the Commissioners of the Land Office to purchase the land on which the Friend's Settlement was located. Parker noted:

> I Expect you will Judge it most for the benefit of the State to let us have these Lands on Easy terms Because our Settlement Consisting of about Sixty familys are settled on & near them, in which Settlement we have a good Grist Mill & Saw mill. And carry on Necessary branches of Business which only a few common families could not due. which makes it easy for one or More families to Settle in our Neighbourhood which otherwise they could not do. which has greatly Incouraged the Settling that part of this State.

Parker made it clear that he was acting under the authorization of, and on behalf of, the community of Universal Friends, which he stated numbered about sixty families. He pleaded for enough land "as may accomodate the aforesaid Number of Familys with Sufficient farms. And also about half that Number More that we Expect will Soon come and Settle among us if there was room for them."

The Land Commissioners acted favorably on Parker's request on May 9, 1791, but even possession of a deed to the land they had settled failed to bring tranquillity to the community of Universal Friends. A new survey of the Pre-emption Line in November and December, 1792, revealed the suspected fraud and placed the actual line some distance to the east. Thus some of the land on which the members of the society had built their homes was not included in the grant from the state, but was, in fact, part of the tract now owned by the absentee British speculators. Wearily a number of Universal Friends appealed to Charles Williamson for the right to purchase the land they had improved. Even some of the settlers whose farms lay within the territory purchased from the state found themselves in jeopardy when a few of the society's leaders sought personal profits at the expense of the community.

By 1791, it was evident that the settlement by Seneca Lake was not to be the realization of Jemima Wilkinson's dreamed-of refuge in the wilderness, where her followers could gather around their spiritual leader and escape the corrupting influences of the material world. The persistent failure to secure a sound title to enough land for all the members of the community discouraged both those who came and other potential settlers back in New England and Pennsylvania. Not only was the available land insufficient to provide self-sustaining farms for the poorer members of the society, but many who had invested both money and years of hard labor found themselves threatened with the loss of their homes. Into neighboring territory, made more valuable by the success of the Friend's Settlement, moved skeptical nonbelievers, often hostile toward the Universal Friends and their way of life. The rapid rise in land values offered an opportunity for wealth that was a greater temptation than some of the Universal Friend's society could resist. Some of the leaders of the society defected, and others became discouraged and left.

One of the most prominent families of the New Milford group of Universal Friends was that of Abraham and Abigail Dayton. When the difficulty over the land title first became evident, Abraham Dayton went to Canada and secured a sizable tract of land from Governor Simcoe. He tried to persuade Jemima Wilkinson to relocate there, but Sarah Richards, who was in poor health, opposed moving so far. When Jemima decided not to move, Dayton sold his interest in the mill on the Outlet to David Wagener in December, 1791, and took his family to Canada. Although he remained steadfast in his regard for the Universal Friend, his removal was a blow to the community.

Less lamentable, but more disruptive to the society, was the loss of James Parker. Parker's failure as a leader should have been recognized much earlier, but no action was taken until October 27, 1791. On that date a meeting was held at his house, and seventeen members who had advanced money to him voted to authorize William Potter and Thomas Hathaway as a committee to take his place in further negotiations for the community's land. Parker was instructed to turn over all the papers relating to the contract with the Governor and Commissioners of the Land Office. To insure him against any loss or damage he was given a bond for one thousand pounds to guarantee faithful performance of the contract by the community, and he was promised a just payment for his services. Potter and Hathaway were also promised a reasonable recompense for their services and were required to give a bond for eight thousand pounds to be "deposited in the hands of the Universal Friend, to be kept for the safety of the Community untill the whole be finished and completed." Members of the community who had given money to James Parker were to be permitted to buy shares in the land expected from the Land Office in proportion to the sums they had already paid. Other members of the community could purchase any shares in the land that remained.

Although Parker could not have been happy at the diminution of his authority, he did not break with the society immediately. Potter and Hathaway paid the Treasurer of New York State one thousand pounds on February 29, 1792, and on October 10, 1792, the Governor issued a patent deeding 14,040 acres to James Parker, William Potter, and Thomas Hathaway, as tenants in common, and not as joint tenants, for themselves and their associates. For one shilling and sixpence an acre, or about eighteen and a half cents, the three patentees received a grant of land worth at least six dollars an acre, considering the improvements of the settlers. Parker was already disgruntled, and Judge William Potter was willing to sacrifice his own position in the Society of Universal Friends for a potential profit of about forty thousand dollars.

Meetings were held in the Friend's Meeting House on May 20, June 11, and August 15, 1793, and a decision was reached to divide the land into twelve classes and apportion shares in the various classes without regard for the homes and farms of the actual settlers. Potter had put up most of the purchase price paid to the state and received nearly half of the property, five-twelfths and a quarter of a twelfth, to be exact, which became known as the Potter location. In vain did Thomas Hathaway protest Potter's purchase of so large a share of the land, and offer money of his own, which Potter refused. Hathaway even made an unsuccessful trip to Albany to complain to the governor that the lands of the grant were not divided among the Universal Friends according to their original intention. Only seventeen persons shared in the actual division, and several who had come with the pioneer party in 1788 received no land at all and even lost the value of their improvements. Greed for land, and the wealth it represented, shattered the unity of the society of Universal Friends as no amount of adverse criticism had been able to do.[2]

Even before the rupture with James Parker and William Potter, Jemima Wilkinson was making plans to escape the insecurity, hostile influences, and conflicts of the Gore. Early in 1794 she moved farther west to plant her New Jerusalem by the waters of Y-shaped Crooked Lake.

Chapter VII

Jerusalem

HER move to Jerusalem was the Universal Friend's last attempt to find a place where "no intruding foot" could enter. Although the settlement in western New York State failed to provide the desired seclusion, it remained her home for the final quarter century of her life. After eighteen years of almost constant travel, forty-four-year-old Jemima Wilkinson settled down to minister to the loyal members of her society, who gathered around her and turned a frontier wilderness into a stable, rural community.

Jerusalem was Township Number Seven of the second range of the Phelps and Gorham purchase. This township, six miles square and containing about 23,040 acres, was purchased by Thomas Hathaway and Benedict Robinson for $10,320, or about forty-five cents an acre. As original shareholders in the Phelps and Gorham purchase, they were entitled to buy the land at prime cost.[1] They explored the township in December, 1789, and Robinson reported what they had found in a letter to Sarah Richards: "The land does not lay as compact as one could wish for," but it was good enough, and the timber exceeded any he had seen "in this or any other country." They were well satisfied. A pleasant stream, with two or more fine mill sites, ran the length of the township from north to south, emptying into the west branch of Crooked Lake. It was given the name Brook Kedron by Thomas Hathaway. Almost all of their purchase could be viewed from a high point of land they called Sheppard's Hill. Robinson expressed his hope that the Universal Friend would accept his previous offer of a piece of land in the new township. This invitation had been made before the Universal Friend had joined the settlement near Seneca Lake, while Parker was still negotiating to get a clear title to the property there.

Although both Hathaway and Robinson were men of independent wealth, they evidently had the interests of the society of Universal Friends in mind when they purchased the township called Jerusalem. Their negotiations with Oliver Phelps were concurrent with Parker's deal with the Lessee Company; they purchased the land even before it became evident that the settlement on the Gore was not the New Jerusalem of Jemima Wilkinson's dreams. Both men were also major investors in the original settlement and received sizable shares when the land in the Gore was divided. On February 19, 1790, Benedict Robinson

signed an agreement to let David Wagener buy a share
of the new township equal to his own and to Hathaway's,
an option that was never exercised. Robinson agreed that
anyone who had previously given money to James Parker
to buy land would have an opportunity to purchase shares
in the new township.[2]

Jerusalem township was surveyed during the summer
of 1791 by Daniel Guernsey, a "practical surveyor" hired
by Robinson. Guernsey and a group of men spent from
the end of June to September 20 dividing the township
into seventy-two lots of about three hundred and twenty
acres each.

In the same year Jemima Wilkinson decided to move
from the Gore. She and Sarah Richards were conducted
by Benedict Robinson on a tour of the township to select
a location for a new home. Sarah preferred a site in the
western part of the township, but Jemima chose the northern section, including part of the valley and stream and a
large hill with a southeastern slope. A deed for fourteen
hundred acres of land was given to Sarah Richards by
Benedict Robinson on January 5, 1792. Although it was
not stated in the deed, it was understood that Sarah Richards was acting as a trustee for the Universal Friend.

This arrangement was necessary because Jemima Wilkinson, from the beginning of her ministry, refused to own
any real property in her own name. Her attitude was
explained in a petition, stating that she, "being wholly
devoted to her Religious Duties & deeming it inconsistent
therewith & unbecoming her character to have any personal concern or agency in pecuniary or temporal concerns constituted Sarah Richards, one of her most Trustworthy Followers & Friends, Trustee of the lands." Sarah

Richards was a logical choice for trustee by virtue of her education and ability as well as her absolute loyalty. She explained her role in a letter to Ruth Prichard on March 12, 1793.

The Friend has got enough land here for all that will be faithful & true. Dear Ruth, I will inform Thee that Bened. Robinson has given the Friend a Deed of some land in the second seventh in the Boston prehemption which Deed contains five lotts and the Friend has made use of my name to hold it in trust for the Friend, and likewise for the poor friends and such as have no helper, where no intruding foot cant enter.

However much Jemima Wilkinson's aloofness from practical, material affairs may have strengthened her position as the spiritual leader of her community, it was the basis for misunderstanding that eventually helped to bring about the decline of that very community. As long as Sarah Richards lived, the Universal Friend's property was in good hands. But Sarah Richards was always in poor health and suffered severely from the rigors of frontier life. When she was able, she joined the Friend in supervising the clearing of the land in Jerusalem and in planning the first log house that was built there. She did not live to move there, however. In July, 1793, she was taken sick and after seventeen weeks of painful illness, in which she was nursed by the Friend, she died on November 30, at the age of thirty-six. Although she made a will leaving the property that she held in trust, to Rachel Malin, the document was drawn up by the doctor from Canandaigua who attended her and contained legal deficiencies that resulted in years of litigation and heartache.

The death of Sarah Friend, her closest companion and

most dependable associate for ten years, was a great personal loss to Jemima Wilkinson. At the funeral services she preached a moving sermon, beginning her exhortation, "It is better to go to the house of mourning than to the house of feasting, for that is the end of all men, and the living will lay it to heart." Her text was from Isaiah 57: 1-2, "The righteous perisheth, and no man layeth it to heart: and merciful men are taken away, none considering that the righteous is taken away from the evil to come. He shall enter into peace: they shall rest in their beds, each one walking in his uprightness." "A great Meeting," reported Ruth Prichard, "This day the Friend told us the time is coming when it will be like a Jubillee Trumpet to have it said, There is Mercy for the Soul."

It was also Ruth Prichard who recorded Jemima Wilkinson's departure from the Gore: "20th. of the 2d. Mo. 1794 The Dear Universal FRIEND Moved from this Settlement." Jemima Wilkinson must have had a heavy heart on that day as she moved into the house in Jerusalem that Sarah Richards had such a large part in planning and building. This New Jerusalem was no golden land of milk and honey. Although the move was no more than a dozen miles west from the Friend's Settlement on Seneca Lake, it meant leaving an established community of comfortable homes and cultivated fields for a completely new start in a virgin wilderness. It was impressive country. The fertile valley of the Brook Kedron was lined on both sides by steep hills and deep gullies, and the whole country was heavily wooded with sugar maple, pine, oak, and walnut. But the beauty of the natural setting could not be appreciated by the early pioneer, who was faced with almost superhuman toil to clear the land and make the soil yield the food he and his family needed for survival. For many of the Universal Friend's followers, the fight to subdue this wilderness was a repetition of their earlier struggle in the Gore. The price of loyalty to the Friend for some of these earliest settlers was additional years of hard labor and sacrifice. Many were willing to pay the price, however, and left the Gore to make their homes near her.

The Universal Friend's first house in Jerusalem was located about a mile south of the northern boundary of the township on the west side of the Brook Kedron. It was a simple log building, to which two log additions were attached, the middle one serving as a meeting room for the society. The first, most easterly, dwelling, the largest of the three, was eventually raised a story higher and the whole building covered with siding, making a comfortable abode. This was Jemima Wilkinson's home for twenty of the twenty-five years she lived in Jerusalem. It could hardly be called luxurious, but the Duc de la Rochefoucauld-Liancourt called it "extremely pretty and commodious" although "built only of the trunks of trees." For looks or comfort it could not compare with the spacious frame mansion built about the same time for Arnold Potter about a mile and a half to the north. The stories circulated by her detractors that Jemima Wilkinson lived in luxury on the frontier while her followers existed under the most primitive conditions are not true. Only when the country had become quite domesticated, after two decades of hard work and planning, was the fine frame house in which she spent the last five years of her life actually completed.

Meanwhile the triple log house was the center of the society as well as the Universal Friend's home. North of the house a road, more accurately described as a trail, ran east over the hills to the settlement at the Gore. In back of the house were log barns, and across the road a large log building served as a workshop where the women of the Friend's household did their carding, spinning, weaving, and sewing. A fine spring to the south of the house furnished drinking water and cooled the springhouse, in which milk, cheese, butter, and meat were stored. East of the house was a garden, "kept in good order." Except that it housed a larger family than was usual, the Universal Friend's house in Jerusalem was not greatly different from other dwellings on the western New York frontier.

As the home of the Publick Universal Friend and her "family," as her household was called, this residence was unique in western New York, however. Although never considered to be communal property, in practice the Friend's house was a home for any of the needy members of the society. From sixteen to eighteen people lived there regularly in addition to whatever guests might be accepting the Friend's hospitality. Most of the Friend's household were women who followed her practice of celibacy. At least fifteen women were members of the Friend's family at one time or another. Closest to Jemima, after the death of Sarah Richards, were Rachel and Margaret Malin. The Malin sisters came from a large family of Philadelphia Quakers. They and two of their brothers, Elijah and Enoch, were disowned by the Society of Friends in 1789 and 1790 for joining Jemima Wilkinson's fellowship. Rachel had been a mantua maker, or seamstress, in Philadelphia, but became the trustee of the Universal Friend's property, succeeding Sarah Richards, and carefully kept the accounts of the Friend's household.

Other members of the household included Chloe Towerhill, a former Negro slave who had joined the Friend's family after gaining her freedom; she was in charge of the kitchen. Mary Bean lived with the Friend from early life and became mistress of the dairy. Henry Barnes came to live in the Friend's family in 1800 at the age of eleven; he worked in the barn, drove the cows, looked after the horses, and guarded the sheep. The youngest member of the family was Eliza Richards, orphaned daughter of Sarah Richards; she was the cause of great trouble for the Friend and her society.

Not all of the celibate women resided in the Friend's house. Many of them had houses or cabins of their own on the Friend's land or lived with families in the vicinity. Although the Universal Friend employed men to clear some of the land and build her house in Jerusalem, from the first poorer members of the society cleared patches of her land and built log houses for themselves with her permission, living there and working the land, rent free. Although such men of wealth as Thomas Hathaway, Sr., and David Wagener were loyal followers until their death, and a number of other followers had money enough to purchase land in Jerusalem, most of those who followed the Universal Friend in this move were the poorer members of the society. They were victims of the confusion over land titles in the Gore and felt themselves injured in the disposition of the land there, many of them losing the fruits of several years of hard work. It is clear that the Universal Friend sympathized with these people and that her move to Jerusalem was, in part, a rebuke to some of the more prosperous members of the society who secured their own estates without regard for their poorer neighbors. This position increased the loyalty of the poorer folk to their beloved leader, but it alienated and embittered others who had the wealth and the power to cause her trouble.

Once she left the settled area of the Gore, the Friend's main concern was making a home for herself and her followers in the wilderness. Until her health began to fail in the last decade of her life, Jemima Wilkinson was an active woman who would not hesitate, on occasion, to take hold of one end of a crosscut saw and help work up a log into firewood. She also hoed and weeded in her garden, picked berries, plucked grass for weaving baskets, and did other chores necessary on a frontier farm. She hired her own help and directed the work on her premises in person, riding through the fields, often accompanied by a boy to lower and put back the fence bars. Although members of the society sometimes worked for her as a voluntary contribution, the account books kept by Rachel Malin show that most of the work done for the Universal Friend was paid for. The story that she appropriated both the labor and the possessions of her followers by the command, "The Friend hath need of that," was always vehemently denied by those who were close to her, and the detailed account books, recording even small sums paid for supplies or labor, support the denial. According to Henry Barnes she would ask for something, and if it could not be done she would say, "What is not, cannot be numbered."

The economic development of Jerusalem paralleled that of other frontier communities. As land was cleared, the trees were burned for potash. Later a sawmill erected on the brook produced boards to build the frame houses that replaced the log cabins. Wheat and rye were sown on the cleared ground, and eventually grassy pastures made it possible to keep cattle and sheep. An important resource was the magnificent sugarbush along the Brook Kedron, which caused a later, less biblical, generation to call the stream Sugar Creek. Here two of the Friend's household, almost unassisted, made over fifteen hundred pounds of maple sugar in the spring of 1816. Gradually the forest was pushed back, and a land of open fields and scattered farms appeared. Rachel Malin described her impression of Jerusalem in a letter to a friend in Philadelphia.

I feel myself happy in exploring those shady groves, for wherever I turn my eyes I find something to invite my curiosity and to engage my attention, for the woods offer their shades, and the fields their harvest and the hills flatter with an extensive view and the valley invites with shelter, fragrance and flowers. Solitude is pleasant to me; this new world is richly adorned with hills and valley. It abounds with almost everything we could wish for.

The Publick Universal Friend presided over this frontier community like the matriarch of a large family. Not only was she the spiritual leader who consoled the bereaved at funerals and preached at the religious services but she ministered in other ways as well. Members of the society came to her for advice and to settle minor disputes. She visited and nursed the sick, skillfully treating illnesses and injuries. When Abigail Dayton suffered a compound fracture in a battle with a black snake, the Friend set and dressed the leg, which healed without difficulty, as Mrs. Dayton loved to testify until her death at the age of ninety-three. In spite of the Friend's attitude on marriage and procreation, she was fond of children, especially girls. She would often hold them in her lap and question them about their conduct or listen to their ABC's.

On Saturday morning, from all over the settlement, the Universal Friends set out for the place of meeting in time to arrive by ten thirty. The men wore low-crowned, broad-brimmed beaver hats and the women poke bonnets of dove-colored silk; the children dressed like their parents. Those who could not attend the services in person sat in their homes and observed a period of silent meditation and prayer. For several years after moving to Jerusalem the Universal Friend returned at regular intervals to hold meetings at the log meetinghouse in the Gore, at David Wagener's house on the site of Penn Yan, or in other homes. On these occasions the Universal Friend and a group from Jerusalem would ride the dozen miles on horseback on Friday afternoon and return on Sunday afternoon.

At Jerusalem the meetings were held in a room of the log house fitted out with several benches arranged in rows. A group usually came over from the Gore on Friday and spent two nights at the Friend's house. At the time of meeting the worshipers entered the room and sat down in silence, the men always wearing their hats in the old Quaker manner. The Universal Friend then came in and took her place at one end of the room, sitting with Rachel Malin on her right and Margaret Malin on her left. She removed her broad-brimmed hat and handed it to Rachel, then knelt and opened the meeting with prayer. After sitting a few minutes in silence she delivered her sermon, based on a text, usually speaking an hour and a half. Once she spoke two and a half hours. It was not the length of the sermons that her congregation remembered, however, but her eloquence. To them her voice was musical and pleasant, never raised above its natural pitch and unadorned

with oratorical effects. Her only gestures were easy waving motions of one hand. She never brought a Bible to her
meetings, although she quoted chapter and verse and
repeated long sections from memory. She told no anecdotes; her only allusions were to the Bible. No singing was
permitted, another old Quaker practice followed by the
Universal Friends. After the Friend's sermon, other members of the society would often rise and speak if the
Spirit moved them. The meeting was dismissed with general handshaking, beginning when the Friend shook hands
with Rachel Malin and continuing until all had shaken
hands with one another and especially with the Friend.

Strangers were more critical of the Universal Friend
as a preacher. The Duc de la Rochefoucauld-Liancourt,
who attended one of her meetings in 1795, observed, "In
point of delivery, she preached with more ease, than any
other Quaker, I have yet heard; but the subject matter of
her discourse was an eternal repetition of the same topics,
death, sin and repentance." He thought that her action
was studied, that, although she aimed at simplicity, there
was something pedantic in her manner. John Lincklaen,
who went to meeting to hear the Universal Friend in 1791,
while she was still in the Gore, was not impressed by her
preaching either: "I sought, but in vain, to find some principles on which she founds her religion, but her sermon
was only a quantity of vain words without sense or reason." Evidently listeners who were inclined to be critical
of Jemima Wilkinson as a person were unimpressed with
her as a preacher, while those who knew her best received inspiration from her discourses.

On Saturday evening, after all who attended the morning meeting had been guests at dinner, it was customary

to hold silent meeting, where the members of the society sat in silent prayer and meditation. Again the Quaker influence is evident. The religious meetings of the society were always open to the public, and no stranger was ever refused hospitality at her home. Even when it was evident that visitors had come only out of curiosity, they were received and fed and treated courteously. Perhaps the most distinguished visitor, and certainly the one whose observations about Jemima Wilkinson attracted the most attention down through the years, was the Duc de la Rochefoucauld-Liancourt. The Duke passed through Jerusalem in June, 1795, on his way from Philadelphia to visit Niagara Falls, a scenic attraction that no one who claimed to be a traveler in the United States could miss. Together with his party of ten, the Duke attended the regular Saturday meeting on June 6, 1795. After the meeting the whole group accepted Jemima's invitation to dinner. "Our plates, as well as the table-linen, were perfectly clean and neat," noted the Duke. "Our repast, although frugal, was yet better in quality than any, of which we had partaken, since our departure from Philadelphia; it consisted of good fresh meat, with pudding, an excellent sallad, and a beverage of a peculiar yet charming flavour." The ten Frenchmen dined in one group and were followed by another of the same number while as many more dined in the kitchen. The Duke was less impressed by the hospitality furnished to such a crowd than by the fact the Universal Friend left to eat in her own room with one of her women companions.[3]

The Duke recorded many of the derogatory stories repeated about Jemima in the interesting and detailed account of his travels, first published in English in 1799. As a man of the Enlightenment, he had little respect for "dervises, pontiffs, and priests of most religious persuasions," whom he considered to be either impostors or enthusiasts. Jemima he classified in the first category. When his own observations are separated from his opinions and from the stories that he picked up by hearsay, however, the Universal Friend appears as an honest and sincere religious fanatic rather than a conscious fraud.

The same image is presented in an account by an anonymous traveler to Niagara Falls in 1812, who was interested enough in Jemima Wilkinson to secure a letter of introduction and to make a special trip from Canandaigua. Although he opened his conversation by confessing that his visit was to gratify his curiosity, he was politely received. He observed, in an account published in *The Christian Disciple* in 1817:

She replied . . . to several questions as to her opinions on particular subjects of theology with sufficient verbosity, with a confused mass of scriptural quotations, and almost always with obscurity, which sometimes was impenetrable. Her command of the contents of the bible, and her readiness in the use of scriptural language were surprising. She used few expressions which could not be found in the sacred books. . . . I could not discover that her opinions differed from those of the Quakers, except that she assumed for herself the honor of a divine appointment, for what special purpose I heard not.

Other travelers made their way over the roads to Jerusalem to see the celebrated Jemima Wilkinson, a legend even before she died. Later described as "the second wonder of the western country," her home seemed to be an essential detour in the grand tour to Niagara Falls. Not all came out of curiosity, however. A son of the William

Hencher from Newton Point who had helped Jemima
Wilkinson through the woods to Catherine's Town in
1790 recalled her kindness and hospitality when the family
had stopped at her residence on their way farther west
to the Genesee River.

Visitors always found her self-possessed and never at
a loss for words. A story that is perhaps apocryphal, but
not at all improbable, relates her answer to a man named
Day, who was trying to induce her to admit to the name
Jemima Wilkinson instead of the Universal Friend. An-
noyed by his insistence, she asked his name, with which
she was already familiar, and on receiving his answer, she
commented, "Day! Day! thy day will soon be turned into
night unless thee mends thy ways." On another occasion,
at the end of a visit from James Wadsworth, the Friend
said to him, "Thou art a lawyer; thou has plead for others;
has thou ever plead for thyself to the Lord?" Mr. Wadsworth replied courteously, and the Friend, requesting those
present to kneel with her, prayed fervently; after which
she rose, shook hands with Mr. Wadsworth, and retired
to her apartment.

The Indian as well as the pioneer enjoyed the hospitality
of the Universal Friend. Indeed, the Indians were her
nearest neighbors for several years. The Friend's Settlement on Seneca Lake was the largest white community by
far in the Genesee country when Jemima Wilkinson first
arrived. One or two families had settled at Catherine's
Town near the head of Seneca Lake, and a few settlers
and Indian traders lived at Kanadesaga (Geneva) at the
foot of the lake. Except for a few scattered traders and
settlers in the country between Seneca Lake and the British
garrison at Fort Niagara, "all else was Seneca Indian oc-

cupancy." Relations between the members of the Universal Friend's society and the original inhabitants of the country were uniformly friendly.

It may be that the Universal Friends benefited originally from the respect and good will felt by the Indians toward the Quakers. Their language, dress, and the designation of their community as the Friend's Settlement might well lead even more sophisticated observers than the Indians to conclude that they were regular Quakers, and in their dealings with the Indians they preserved the Quaker reputation for scrupulous fairness. As the Indians signed away their lands in a series of treaties, they gradually moved farther west, but for many years a few Indian families squatted here and there among the cabins of the white settlers, and groups of Indians roamed their ancestral hunting grounds. Often demoralized by liquor, these scattered remnants of a great people were objects of curiosity to the traveler and were frequently exploited by the whites. No liquor was sold by Jemima's followers, however, and at her home and at those of the members of her society the Indian visitor was treated with the same respect shown any other guest.

Five or six hundred of the Senecas camped by Seneca Lake not far from the Friend's house in June 1791. This group, which one pioneer settler remembered as including squaws, papooses, dogs, and even pigs, was on its way to meet Commissioner Timothy Pickering for a council at Newtown. The leaders of this band included the famous orator, Red Jacket, the preacher, Good Peter, and Cornplanter. Such a congregation so near at hand offered the Universal Friend an opportunity that she could not miss. Going to the Indian camp, she delivered a sermon that was received with polite attention. Good Peter also preached on the same occasion. It was characteristic of the Iroquois tribes, whose social structure was matriarchal and whose sachems were chosen by the matrons, for a woman to be received respectfully.

The most important of the Indian councils in western New York was held in Canandaigua in the fall of 1794. Colonel Timothy Pickering again represented the United States. A delegation of Quakers, including William Savery, came from Philadelphia at the invitation of the Indians, who had in mind the Quaker's reputation for fairness. Savery had a low opinion of Jemima Wilkinson, but he rode over from Canandaigua to Jerusalem to see her, spending the night at Judge William Potter's on the way. He reported Judge Potter's disillusionment with the Universal Friend and Potter's feeling of having suffered financially from association with her society. Savery, an experienced Quaker missionary, did his best to talk down the Universal Friend but complained that "her assurance, and artful manner of leading off from a subject which she did not relish, rendered our efforts abortive." In his failure to break down Jemima Wilkinson's poise and confidence, William Savery was in good company. This woman of no formal education could hold her own in verbal dueling with any of her visitors, including clergymen. Savery contented himself with the comment that nothing short of divine power could bring her to "a state of reason or christianity" and predicted a rapid decline for her society. However, he did record the role that Jemima Wilkinson played in the great Indian council at Canandaigua.

The progress at the council in the fall of 1794 was slow. British officials and exiled Tories operated from Fort

Niagara and Fort Oswego to encourage Iroquois hostility. Savery observed upon coming to Canandaigua, "As the Indians are all round, and the settlement of the whites very thin, there still is some danger to be apprehended." He might have added that the followers of Jemima Wilkinson had lived in this territory for six years, increasing in number from twenty-five to several hundred without a single unpleasant incident with the Indians. Farther west Indian hostility was serious until General Anthony Wayne's decisive victory at Fallen Timbers. News of the defeat of their western brothers was an important factor in counteracting British intrigue and in convincing the Six Nations of the Iroquois to agree to the Pickering treaty.

In October, while the negotiations were still under way, Jemima Wilkinson and a party including Rachel Malin, David Wagener, and Enoch Malin came to Canandaigua. They dined at Thomas Morris' house at the invitation of Colonel Pickering and attended the council. After listening to several speeches, the Universal Friend and all her company kneeled and prayed. Requesting permission to speak, she addressed the council with what Savery described as "many texts of scripture, without much similarity or connexion." According to the account of her followers, however, her sermon text was Malachi 2:10, "Hath we not all one father? hath not one God created us?" Certainly this sentiment correctly described her attitude toward the Indians and may explain her good relations with them. The tradition is that the Indians were greatly pleased with her discourse and gave her the name Squaw *Shinnewawna gis tau, ge*—"A Great Woman Preacher."

The next day three Indian women, introduced by Red Jacket, spoke to the council. The white people were the cause of the Indian distresses, they declared. "One of the white women had yesterday told the Indians to repent; and they now called on the white people to repent, for they had as much need as the Indians." By this time Jemima Wilkinson had returned home, but had she been present she certainly would have supported the call of the Indian women. Her pleas for repentance were directed to all races and levels of society. The answer to the Indian women gave Colonel Pickering an opportunity to make some gallant but condescending remarks about women. The woman preacher had spoken without his approval, he declared. She forced herself into the council contrary to his advice, "but as she was a woman, he was tender of her." It was well that the Universal Friend was not present to express her reaction to such solicitude. At least some of the contemporary resentment toward the Universal Friend for her success as a preacher and leader of a religious society was based on the fact that she was a woman. Others agreed with the lad who remembered the Universal Friend in her unusual dress as she came through Newtown Point on her way to the first settlement because it seemed so strange to see "a woman controlling and directing men in all things appertaining to the journey." It seemed to him a "one woman power."

Pickering's treaty of 1794 at Canandaigua was followed by peace with the Iroquois and renewed settlement in western New York. After the British garrisons surrendered Fort Niagara and Fort Oswego under the terms of the Jay treaty, the area had peace and security until the War of 1812. Neither the attempts of British Governor Simcoe to discourage American settlement on the lands of the Iroquois nor the intrigues of the associates of the Lessee Company to form a separate state were successful. The largest group of Americans in the area during this critical period was the colony founded by Jemima Wilkinson. Her early success in bringing substantial numbers into the region attracted other pioneers and made subsequent settlement easier. The Genesee country would have been settled eventually, but the decision of the Universal Friend to locate her New Jerusalem there brought loyal Americans into the region at a critical time. Not the least significant of Jemima Wilkinson's roles is the part she played in encouraging the settlement of western New York and in helping to secure this disputed region to the United States.

Chapter VIII

Trials and Tribulations

AFTER the Publick Universal Friend settled in western New York, few new converts were added to her society, and it began a steady decline in numbers. Some of the wealthiest and most respected of its members defected and turned against their former leader with the bitterness characteristic of apostates. The younger members of the society, the second generation of the original settlers, rejected the austerity of the Friend's leadership and ultimately her authority. The effectiveness of Jemima Wilkinson's magnetic attraction seemed to diminish as her youthful beauty succumbed to the advance of middle age, but her self-confidence never waned. In spite of assaults on her property, attacks on her character, and the transition of trusted friends to active enemies, the Publick Universal Friend showed neither bitterness nor discouragement. Even the collapse of her dream of a community of the faithful, free from the "intruding foot," did not shake her faith in her mission.

Many factors contributed to the failure of the plan for a secluded community separated from the world. The Universal Friends selected too promising a region to hold a monopoly on it, and from the beginning community solidarity was weakened by outsiders. The selection of James Parker as leader of the settlement was unfortunate. Had Parker been successful in the beginning in getting a clear title to two or three townships at the original low price for which they were sold, there would have been land enough to provide even the smallest shareholder with a suitable farm. Instead, his ill-advised bargain-hunting with the Lessee Company and the shifts in the Pre-emption Line cost the society dearly. The rapid increase in land values caused by speculation incited the greed of both Parker and William Potter. Although Parker was a man whose ambition outran his ability for leadership and whose personality did not inspire popular confidence, his defection after fourteen years as a leader of the society must have shaken the confidence of other members. Furthermore, Parker, who had been a justice of the peace in Rhode Island and a Revolutionary officer, was appointed justice of the peace of Ontario County, and he used his new position to harass his former coreligionists and their leader. An even greater loss to the society, because of their social position and prestige as well as financial resources, was Judge William Potter and his son, Arnold. Arnold Potter became a judge of the Ontario County court, and his home, only a mile and a half north of the Friend's house in Jerusalem, was long a center of hostility toward the Universal Friend.[1]

The Universal Friend's injunction on celibacy, although not strictly enforced, caused some defections and probably explains the loss to the society of many of the sons and daughters of the original members. One such defector, Benedict Robinson, was one of the most devoted followers of Jemima Wilkinson from the early days in Rhode Island, joining the society when he was in his early twenties and traveling with her on many of her trips. With Thomas Hathaway he made the purchase of Jerusalem Township and helped the Universal Friend establish herself there. Robinson was one of the original settlers, whose contribution had been sufficient to provide him with a comfortable estate in the Gore. He lived alone and had as a housekeeper Susannah Brown, who lived nearby with her sister Temperance.

Early one morning in 1792, according to a popular story, Thomas Hathaway came to Benedict's house on business and found Colonel Charles Williamson there. Williamson, who informed him that Benedict was not well and was still in bed, led Hathaway upstairs to find Benedict in bed with Susannah. "Good Lord! Benedict, what does this mean?" exclaimed the horrified Thomas. "Why, Benedict got tired of sleeping alone, and crept in bed with Susannah," explained Williamson. Only later, after Thomas had left to inform the Friend, did Williamson explain his joke. As justice of the peace, he had just married the two, with Temperance Brown, Barnabus Brown, and Elnathan Botsford—all members of the Friend's society—as witnesses. Al-

though it is doubtful whether Jemima Wilkinson found
any humor in the crude joke, she accepted this marriage
as she had many others in the society. Robinson, however,
experienced a gradual disillusionment with the spiritual
leadership of the Universal Friend and for a while was a
leader in the group of enemies that harassed her. After
several years of bitter hostility he became reconciled and
returned to her meetings in Jerusalem, apparently forgiven.[2]

The greatest threat to the Universal Friend's material
possessions also grew out of a revolt against the prohibition
on marriage. An elopement from the Friend's own household resulted in a challenge that threatened her own home
and the homes of many of her followers in Jerusalem.
Blonde, blue-eyed Eliza Richards grew up in the Friend's
household from early childhood. She was left often in the
care of the Universal Friend and Ruth Prichard, who
tutored her while her mother, Sarah Richards, traveled on
behalf of the Friend. When Sarah Richards died, Eliza
was left a ward of the Universal Friend. A few months
later the thirteen-year-old girl was moved from the settlement at the Gore to the wilderness of Jerusalem. As Eliza
grew to young womanhood, she caught the eye of Enoch
Malin, about ten years her senior, who was the younger
brother of Rachel and Margaret. Since a normal courtship
would have been impossible under the doctrine of the Universal Friend, Eliza eloped in 1796 at the age of sixteen.
On a sabbath, while all were in meeting and the Universal
Friend was preaching, she climbed out the window of the
Friend's bedroom, took the horse that had been her mother's from the barn, and rode off with Enoch Malin, to be
married by James Parker, justice of the peace. At first the

Friend refused to admit that Eliza, who was like a daughter, had eloped, believing that Enoch had kidnapped her. This was one marriage that Jemima, who maintained Eliza had been "enticed away" by Enoch, could not accept.

Enoch Malin, "a rolicking fellow, somewhat addicted to drink, but not naturally a bad hearted man," was a carpenter and mill builder by trade, and even tried his hand at keeping a tavern in the Gore, without much success. He soon hit upon a way to improve his fortune by raiding the property of the Universal Friend. In the eyes of the law at that time, any property of a married woman belonged to her husband. Young Eliza Richards Malin had very little property of her own, but she was the only daughter and heir of Sarah Richards, and Sarah Richards had been the trustee and legal owner of all the Universal Friend's land.

Since Enoch always lacked judgment in business matters and Eliza was only "a giddy girl" in her teens, it is not clear how they hit upon the idea of laying claim to the Friend's lands, or whether, as charged, they were instigated to do so. For years both had been intimately associated with the Universal Friend and both were well aware that Sarah Richards held the property in Jerusalem in her name only as a trustee. From a legal standpoint, however, the trust was created in a loose and imperfect manner, and Sarah Richard's will contained defects that would catch the eye of a trained lawyer. At stake was a tract of some 4,500 acres of land, much of it improved, worth from $50,000 to $100,000.[3] Such a rich prize captured the interest of Elisha Williams, a lawyer from Hudson, New York, formerly connected with the ill-fated Lessee Company and involved in other land speculations in western New York.

He became the dominant influence in the legal maneuvers instituted in the names of Enoch and Eliza Malin and, after their deaths, in the names of their two children. Associated with Williams was Robert W. Stoddard of Geneva, whose law partner was David Hudson. Before the legal battle was over, all the principals in the case—Jemima Wilkinson, Enoch and Eliza Malin—were dead; thousands of dollars were expended in litigation; and the assaults of those who coveted her lands had warped the public image of the Universal Friend and her followers almost beyond recognition.

The move against the Universal Friend came within two years after the elopement. In May, 1798, William Carter wrote Richard Smith from Albany that he had heard that Enoch Malin had brought an ejectment action for the whole of Sarah Richards' lands. Carter feared the Universal Friend would not recover before a jury in Ontario County, and recommended an appeal to the Court of Chancery showing that Sarah Richards was only a trustee and that the land in question was never her property. He repeated an earlier suggestion that the society should have a formal organization and trustees. The Universal Friend, however, did not believe in taking disputes to the courts; wishing to avoid legal proceedings, she took no immediate action against Enoch and Eliza.

In fact, she seems to have made no objection when Elnathan Botsford, Jr., and his brother, Benajah, occupied four hundred acres of her land by virtue of a deed purchased from Enoch Malin for $1,200. In August, 1799, Elnathan Botsford, Sr., went to see Jemima, at the request of his sons, to ask her if she had any objections to their purchasing the land from Enoch Malin. Several witnesses remembered that she made no claim to the land and had no

Jemima Wilkinson's last home in Jerusalem, occupied from 1814 until her death in 1819. Construction of the house, begun in 1809, was not completed until 1815.

The Friend's House in Jerusalem as it looks today after restoration. Photograph by Floyd Tillman.

William ~ Aldrich, in Hopewell
~ing to this New settlement, Schen-
ctady. Died. He was aged 85. Went away
in the work of his testifying 18th of
the 5. 11th 1794. His dying testimony he
other matters). But that He said The
Universal Friend, was a Messenger sent
from God.

Candace Heany, left time 9th of
the 3d 11th 1791. aged 45~ The in-
Her last moments calld out My
Friend My Friend And while
The Friend was Praying The
departed. And left evidence of
Faith unfeined. ——

Anna Brown, left time 16th of the 4
11th 1791 aged ~ This was her last
to the Friends desiring them to mind the
Friend. And also to their eternal We were
and was last stepping up her hand. She
Recd. this After which she expired. And
And it appears, went Home in peace.
Were many I feel good ~

Ephraim Macoy, left time,
6th of the 10 e H 1789:

Huldah Andrus, left time
14th of the 11th Mo 1796. aged

Lucy Holmes, left time
of the 8th Mo 1790. She [ ] the
Land of God. Believing in the Day she
visitated. She went away rejoicing giving
glory to God and the Lord this 8th 1790
Vast, at the aweful and mortal life went
clearly Given up her hands in [ ]
glory to God in the highest and that the
Lord [ ] I [ ] [with] me
explain which no mortal [ ]
Quietly looking of the Friend My
Dear Redeemer I love Thee I love Thee;
The [ ]

objection to the Botsfords' buying it. In fact she remarked that she would rather the Botsford family "would buy it and, come and live on it and be neighbors to her than anybody else."

But when Enoch continued to sell deeds to the land for what was described as "trifling consideration" to people less acceptable to the Universal Friend, she began to protest. Against his father's advice, Asahel Stone, Jr., bought the title to fifty acres for $200 in 1805. In 1806 Asa Ingraham paid $250 for a deed to sixty-two and a half acres, then later sold his rights to Truman Stone and moved to Upper Canada. Not until 1811, however, did Jemima Wilkinson begin legal action to protect her property. In June of that year Rachel Malin, as trustee for the Universal Friend, filed a bill in Chancery against Enoch and Eliza Malin and those who purchased from them. The case did not come to a hearing before Chancellor James Kent until November, 1816. At that time, after urgent persuasion by her lawyers, Jemima Wilkinson consented to have her name inserted as a party complainant rather than see the case lost, and the Chancellor allowed the addition. Refusing to decide the case under the rules of equity, the Chancellor directed a feigned issue to be tried before a jury in Ontario County to decide several important questions of fact, including whether Jemima Wilkinson had advanced any money or valuable consideration to Benedict Robinson for the land deeded to Sarah Richards, and whether or not Sarah Richards' will had been altered.

Enoch and Eliza Malin, whose romantic elopement opened the door to the assault on the Universal Friend's home and land, were both dead by this time. They had sold their claim to the property held by Sarah Richards to

Elisha Williams on July 8, 1812, for $1,000 and moved to
Lower Canada. Cut off from family and friends, they wan-
dered about until Enoch Malin, who could always find
work as a skilled carpenter, died and left Eliza with two
small sons and no means of support. She "intermarried or
lived with one Jabe or Jabez Brunson," until she came to
the end of a pathetic life on November 12, 1815, only
thirty-five years old. Elisha Williams was encouraged by
Chancellor Kent's decision and made the next move in
May, 1817, by instituting actions of ejectment against the
Universal Friend, Rachel Malin, and twelve other members
of the society who lived on the Friend's domain. The ejectment case came before the same circuit of the court in Ontario County in June, 1817, at which the trial on the feigned
issue was scheduled. The jury in the ejectment case gave
the verdict to Elisha Williams on the grounds that Sarah
Richards' will, leaving the property of the Universal Friend
to Rachel Malin, was invalid because it had been altered
by some unknown person. Rachel Malin's lawyers then
put off trial on the feigned issue for "lack of a material witness." A new trial was ordered, but before it could be held
Jemima Wilkinson and the thirteen others involved in the
ejectment action filed a complaint in the Court of Chancery, and Chancellor Kent issued an injunction against the
ejectments in 1817.

More than ten years of litigation, ejectments, depositions,
hearings, trials, and uncertainty had elapsed since Enoch
Malin first began to try to raise money by selling the lands
of the Universal Friend, and a final decision was still ten
years away. For the last decade of her life, even in her
final illness, Jemima Wilkinson lived under the threat that
she and the loyal followers who were dependent upon her

might lose their homes and their means of livelihood. Her death in 1819 did not diminish Elisha Williams' determination to have the property, now held by Rachel and Margaret Malin for the Friend's "family" and the poor members of the society of Universal Friends. A hearing of the case was held in June, 1823, before Chancellor Kent, who announced his decision on July 11, only a few days before his retirement. Sarah Richards had held the land in trust for the Universal Friend, the Chancellor decreed, and confirmed the right of the Malin sisters to the property. Elisha Williams appealed to the new Chancellor, Nathan Sanford, on August 4, 1823, and, when Sanford concurred in Chancellor Kent's decision, appealed both these decrees to the Court of Errors, the highest appellate court in the state, consisting of the President of the Senate, the senators, the Chancellor, and judges of the Supreme Court. A lengthy, detailed decision by the Court of Errors, reached in December, 1828, finally terminated the case in favor of the Malin sisters and the society of Universal Friends.[4]

Representing the interests of the Universal Friend were some of the best lawyers in the state. The principal counsel for Jemima and the Malin sisters over the years was Thomas R. Gold of Whitesboro. Gold was at one time an Assistant Attorney General of the state, served in the state Senate and Assembly, and was a member of Congress for three terms. He visited the Universal Friend in Jerusalem at least once, and his letters indicate a personal interest in her and in the Malin sisters. Abraham Van Vechten argued the Friend's case before several courts. The first lawyer admitted to practice under the state constitution, Van Vechten was known as "the father of the New York bar." He served several terms in the state Senate and Assembly, was

Attorney General of the state, and played a leading role in the state constitutional convention of 1821. His prestige and the respect with which he was regarded, as well as his effectiveness in presenting his arguments, undoubtedly helped to win the case for the Malin sisters in the Court of Errors. Another attorney who represented the Universal Friend was John C. Spencer—son of the distinguished Ambrose Spencer—who began his career as a young lawyer in Canandaigua. Spencer rose rapidly in politics, serving in several state offices and in Congress and ultimately becoming Secretary of War and Secretary of the Treasury. He was considered "one of the ablest lawyers of his day." Such legal talent was expensive, and the cost of litigation was a drain on the resources of the Universal Friend and her society.

On the opposite side was Elisha Williams, also one of the most successful lawyers in the state. Williams was a member of the Assembly several times, the recognized leader of the Federalist party in the state, and led the anti-democratic forces in the constitutional convention of 1821. A brilliant orator, he accumulated a large fortune through his law practice and judicious investments, principally in western New York real estate. Ostensibly representing Enoch and Eliza Malin, and later their infant children, Williams was actually working on his own behalf after purchasing Enoch's and Eliza's interests in 1812.

It was "a case involving no difficult or even doubtful question of law, but embarrassed with a multitude of witnesses and a mass of contradictory testimony to an extent which I have seldom known before," Justice Sutherland remarked. Jemima Wilkinson's position was that Sarah Richards never owned the property in question but simply held it in trust for the Universal Friend, a trust which she transferred in her will to Rachel Malin. Acknowledgment that Sarah Richards was acting as a trustee on behalf of the Universal Friend was shown in letters she wrote, receipts she signed, a journal she kept, and the testimony of several persons who heard her state her position in their presence. Considering Sarah Richard's complete devotion to the Universal Friend, a devotion that caused her to leave her only child and to undertake difficult journeys and missions in spite of persistent ill health, Elisha Williams and his associates were hard put to break down the concept of a trust.

Their real hope lay in discrediting the Universal Friend as a fraud and her followers as fanatics completely under her control. To this end they waged a systematic campaign. They charged that Sarah Richards' letters and journal were forged by Ruth Prichard. The testimony of members of the Friend's society ought not to be taken into consideration because of "their faith, their fanaticism and their interest," declared Elisha Williams in court. Outside court Robert W. Stoddard and a group of residents of Jerusalem and the Gore, including some of those who hoped to get part of the Friend's land, sought to discredit the witnesses for the Universal Friend. The names of these persons were given in a series of depositions made in 1824 identifying the combination that spread reports that John Briggs, the clerk of the society, would swear to whatever the Friend told him. Another charge was that Sarah Richards' will was altered after her death, although Moses Atwater, the physician from Canandaigua who attended her in her last illness and drew it up for her testified that it was the same as he drew it. Chancellor Kent's decision on this point was that even if alterations had been made they were not material. The real issue involved was whether or not the Universal Friend and her associates would conspire to use forgery and perjury to hold on to property not legally theirs.

In an attempt to influence public opinion to accept this picture of the Universal Friend and her followers, David Hudson of Geneva, law partner of Robert W. Stoddard, wrote a biography of Jemima Wilkinson. *The History of Jemima Wilkinson, a Preacheress of the Eighteenth Century* was published in Geneva, New York, in 1821, two years after Jemima's death, six years before the litigation over her property was resolved. In it, all the derogatory stories in circulation about her were repeated, many with new embellishments. The surviving members of the Friend's society either chose not to try to refute the book or lacked the ability to write a more accurate account of their leader's life. Hudson's small book, reprinted in Bath in 1844, has been the only biography of Jemima Wilkinson in print and for years was the most easily available source of information about her. Although its obviously hostile approach warned some readers, Hudson's account of ordinary events in the life of his subject was generally accepted as fact. Yet when Hudson's use of names, dates, and noncontroversial incidents are compared with authentic contemporary sources, their inaccuracy is revealed in almost every case. Hudson's book should be considered properly not as a biography of Jemima Wilkinson, but as part of the campaign to get her land by discrediting her aims and aspersing her followers.[5]

Another early effort to destroy the influence of Jemima Wilkinson was an attempt to indict her for blasphemy. This originated with James Parker and Judge William Potter after they became estranged from the society. In the fall of 1799 Parker, as a magistrate of Ontario County, issued a warrant for the arrest of Jemima Wilkinson on the charge of blasphemy. The first attempt to serve the warrant failed when the officer attempted to seize her as she was riding with Rachel Malin in the Gore. The Friend turned her horse, rode down a hill, and reached the home of Richard Smith, where her pursuer was turned away. A second attempt was made by the constable and his assistant at her home in Jerusalem. The two men found Jemima and the women of her household in the workshop but when they attempted to enter, the women flew at them, tore their clothes, and drove them out of doors.

Careful preparations were made for the next attempt. A posse of about thirty men, including Enoch Malin and Eliphalet Norris, bringing an oxcart to carry her away, surrounded the house after midnight. Daniel Brown, Jr., broke down the door with an ax, and they took possession of the premises. Dr. Fargo, who came with the group, warned them, however, that the Friend's health would not permit her to be taken away, and his advice prevailed in spite of a recommendation from Benedict Robinson to "throw her in the cart and carry her off." An agreement was finally reached that the Universal Friend would appear before the next session of the Ontario Circuit Court, and the plan of a trial before Justice Parker was abandoned.

In June, 1800, the Universal Friend, surrounded by loyal followers, rode over the hills to Canandaigua to face her accusers. The case was presented to a grand jury but, blasphemy being held by the presiding judge not to be an indictable offense, it was dismissed. The account in Cleveland's *History of Yates County*, added:

When this conclusion was announced, the Friend was respectfully invited to preach before the Court and people in attendance. She did so, and was listened to with the deepest attention. Judge Spencer, on being asked his opinion of the discourse replied: "We have heard good counsel, and if we live in harmony with what that woman has told us, we shall be sure to be good people here, and reach a final rest in Heaven."

Cleveland was mistaken, however, in identifying the presiding judge as "the venerable Ambrose Spencer." Not until 1804 did Ambrose Spencer become a justice of the Supreme Court. Thomas Morris' identification of the judge in the case as Morgan Lewis, Supreme Court justice from 1792 to 1801, and later Governor of the state, seems more reliable.

Thomas Morris, son of financier Robert Morris, lived in one of the finest houses in Canandaigua. His wife, Sally Kane Morris, inspired by curiosity, invited Jemima Wilkinson to dinner when the Friend came to Canandaigua for the blasphemy trial. Socialite Sally Morris found the Publick Universal Friend "embarrassed and illiterate in her language and awkward in manner." Jemima's comment, after walking through the spacious mansion was, "It was not Heaven after all."

The systematic harassment of the Universal Friend by those who sought to justify their own selfishness or who wanted to secure some of her property undoubtedly weakened her society. But another factor was the failure to develop any real organization or doctrine that would be distinctive enough to retain the loyalty of her followers when her physical energies and the force of her personality began to decline. The old-fashioned virtues of simplicity and self-denial, the preoccupation with death and rewards of heaven, and the stern warnings against the temptations of the material world had little appeal to the next generation. Many of the second generation were interested in enjoying the fruits of their parents' labor. They had farms to run, homes to improve, and families of their own to raise. The world in which they lived was much too pleasant to spoil by introspective concern with sin and worries about salvation.

Abraham Wagener, after the death of his father, would deck his horses out with bells, hitch them to a sleigh filled with young ladies, and drive from Penn Yan out to the Friend's meetings in Jerusalem. He enjoyed the cross, sour looks he got from Jemima. Other young people went to the services that Methodist, Baptist, and Presbyterian itinerant preachers were conducting in Penn Yan and vicinity. Thomas Smith, a Methodist circuit rider, invaded the Friend's domain in February, 1806. He wrote:

At the request of some, I preached a sermon in the green woods near her dwelling, exposing her system and doctrine. . . . Many attended this meeting. It was the largest concourse of people I have seen in this country. On this subject I said all I could, and closed the meeting, while the multitudes disappeared, and Jemima's disciples gather around her to rehearse what they could to her. She wept, and then put the black mark of reprobation on me.

The defections of fellow members of the society and the

opposition of outsiders only seemed to strengthen the
loyalty of those who remained faithful. In her old age, as
in her youth, she was served with affection by a group
of devoted disciples, and ministered to a sizable congregation living in Jerusalem and the Gore.

Chapter IX

Death of a Prophetess

AS the Universal Friend approached threescore years, ill health made it increasingly difficult for her to carry on her active program, but she continued to minister to her small society. Some changes in her daily life were necessary, however. In 1810 the running gear of a carriage she had in Pennsylvania, which had been stored away for the many years that the roads were too poor for such a vehicle, was taken to Canandaigua and fitted with a new body. A traveler passing through the village, noted:

At a coach-maker's in *Canandarque,* as it is spelled on the map, I saw a coachee finishing for JEMIMA, the universal friend, as she calls herself; which one of her avant-couriers or followers-after, was waiting to transport to Crooked Lake, the seat of her abominations. On each side pannel was a star, and on the rear of the carriage a cross of six or eight inches, surmounted by a star with the letters U. F. on each side of the cross. I saw this woman many years since; she was then young and handsome; she is neither now.

Her new carriage, fine as it was, was a reminder that the Universal Friend at fifty-eight was indeed no longer young and could not endure the long rides on horseback that she once enjoyed. She must have felt much sad regret as she gave up her white leather and blue velvet sidesaddle with its silver stirrups for the more comfortable coach. In it she continued to visit the homes of her followers and to get about, addressing meetings at various places and preaching at funerals.

The Universal Friend always believed that funerals offered an ideal situation to dramatize her message of the transitory nature of this earthly life and the necessity of immediate repentance. The Death Book kept by Ruth Prichard Spencer carefully recorded the names and ages of those in the society who "left time" and usually included their "dying words." Fifteen-year-old Candace Keeny "in Her last moments, Called out My Friend! My Friend! And while The Friend was Praying, She departed: And left an evidence of Faith unfained." When faithful Mehitable Smith left time in 1793, the Universal Friend held the funeral meeting at the house, preaching from Isaiah 57:1-2:

At the grave, Friend said, This is the end of all men; and the living will lay it to heart. They that obey are the living. Before the burying I heard the Friend by the Corps repeat this,

> The eyes that Seldom could close,
> With Sorrows forbidden to sleep;
> Seald up in eternal repose,
> Have strangely forgotten to weep

And the Friend Said Precious in the Sight of the Lord is the Death of his Saints.

The Universal Friend's concern for her people is evident in the frequent entries in the Death Book noting "The Friend was with her at the last," and "The Friend closed his eyes," and "A Great Sermon this Day; after which The Dear Friend attended the burying of the Corpse which was decently laid in the silent earth." Her funeral sermons were highly appropriate for each individual. "Lydia Hunt was suddenly snatch'd out of Time, perhaps one hours warning; and then a disembody'd Spirit!—The Friend attended the Solemnity of the funeral and Preach'd from these words Watch Ye! Therefore; For Ye Know not what hour your Lord doth Come!"

The Friend's sense of showmanship, evidenced in her distinctive costume, was evident even in the presence of death. Her coach with its distinctive insignia was unusual enough to attract attention wherever she traveled and to remind observers that the Universal Friend was still "in time," still preaching her message of repentance and salvation. Had she lived in a more modern age, she might well, like Aimee Semple McPherson, have ridden in to her meetings on a white motorcycle.

In spite of the shadow of the litigation that clouded the last years of her life and drained away much of the money earned on the Friend's estate, plans were made for a new building that would be more suitable as a home for her and her household, and as a center of the society. The location selected was near the top of a hill to the west of the house by the Brook Kedron. Thomas Clark of Philadelphia, brother-in-law of Rachel and Margaret Malin and a skillful builder, began construction in 1809. Although the Universal Friend and her family moved into the house on May 20, 1814, it was not completely finished until the next year, requiring six years to build.

The large, three-story, rectangular building is still standing, and resembles a New England farmhouse in style. The simplicity of its exterior is broken by an abundance of windows and three identical paneled doors centered on the south, east, and west sides. Over each door is a semicircular window and a carefully carved pediment. From across the valley, the many windows of the house give the illusion of a flat surface without perspective, like a Grandma Moses painting. Inside, on the first floor, four large rooms, each with a fireplace, flank a central hall that runs the width of the building from east to west. The second floor, also with four large rooms and a central hall, is reached by a simple, graceful stairway. According to tradition the landing of this stairway was so placed that the Universal Friend could stand on it and preach to a congregation seated in both the downstairs and upstairs hallways. The Universal Friend's own bedroom was on the second floor in the southeast corner of the house. From it is a striking view down the valley to the west branch of Keuka Lake. A third floor, containing six smaller rooms, was for members of the household. A deep basement and an attic complete the impressive structure.[1]

During the lifetime of Jemima Wilkinson, the great house was the center of a cluster of service buildings. Back of the house was a two-storied work building where cheese was made on the first floor and spinning and weaving done on the second. Across the road to the east were barns, sheds, and a carriage house. An old-fashioned formal garden was located to the west of the house. No trace of these now remains. The present barn north of the house was not built until long after the Friend was gone. Still standing, however, just southeast of the house is a brick mausoleum built into the hillside. An earlier vault, west of the first house in Jerusalem, held the bodies of James Hathaway, Thomas Hathaway, Sr., and a General William Wall. When it collapsed while being repaired, the bodies were interred in what was known as the Friend's Burying Ground, about a half mile south of her second house, just before the hill plunges downward into a gully. The second vault was intended as the Friend's tomb, but was never used for this purpose.

The spacious mansion provided ample room for the meetings of the society and the same open-handed hospitality that characterized the house under the hill. A separate meetinghouse for the society was planned. Seven hundred and four dollars was collected by James Brown, Jr., and David Wagener gave a piece of land as a building site. But after the timber was hewn and drawn to the lot, the project had to be abandoned because of the expensive litigation over the Universal Friend's estate.

About 1810, James Brown, Jr., became superintendent of the Universal Friend's estate. Born in Lyme, Connecticut, in 1777, he came to the Friend's Settlement about 1792 with his parents and a large number of uncles, aunts, and cousins. He joined the Friend's household and eventually became the most important man in the society, as the

Universal Friend and Rachel and Margaret Malin came to
depend upon him more and more to supervise the work and
handle the details of business.

Although few new members joined the society in the
last years before Jemima Wilkinson's death, the older members drew closer to the Universal Friend to show their
loyalty and affection as her health began to fail. Visitors
also continued to come to try to find some explanation of
the secret of this remarkable woman. A neighbor, not of
the society, who visited her often in the last six years of
her life, confessed, "In frequent conversations with her, I
have sought to draw out her peculiar tenets, and to form a
correct idea of her doctrines. This, however, I have found
was not an easy task. To each question, she always replied
by multiplied quotations of scripture texts, and *by recounting visions;* leaving me to draw inferences to suit myself."

Visions and dreams seemed to occupy much of the time
of the Universal Friend now that she was no longer as active as she had been. Mystical experiences, divinations, and
prophecies had interested her since her own dramatic call
in 1776. One of her dramatic prophecies concerned
Thomas Hathaway, Sr. The elder Hathaway was always
one of the Universal Friend's most loyal followers, although his children were foremost in the ranks of her
enemies after his death. He was one of those who received
a substantial piece of land in the Gore, but left it to move
to Jerusalem, locating his log house there about two miles
south of that of the Friend. The week before he died, he
attended the Friend's meeting, and during her discourse, it
was reported, she turned to him and said, "Thomas, put
thy house in order for thou shalt not live through this
week." Then, while erecting the frame of a sawmill, he was

taken sick with fever and died soon after, on the twenty-fifth of that month.

When La Rochefoucauld-Liancourt visited her in 1795, she gave him a book of prophecies by the Rev. Christopher Love. Christopher Love was a seventeenth-century Royalist conspirator, arrested, tried, and executed by Cromwell. While in the Tower of London just before his death, he made a series of predictions about the future of England and the world which were published and which toward the end of the eighteenth century seemed to be coming true with amazing accuracy. They were reprinted in America in several editions and were much discussed among people who liked to interpret the book of Daniel.

Although none of the surviving papers of the Universal Friend show any evidence of special interest in bibliomancy, they include page after page of recorded dreams and visions. Not only the Friend's dreams, but those of various members of the society, were carefully recorded. Rachel Malin kept a book of dreams in which she noted: "The 10 of the 9 Mo 1815 the Friend dreamed that there was a great woman head brought to the Friend and it taulked with the Friend and sed that it was agoen to have its body again." "The 26 of the 10 Mo 1816 The Friend dreamed that everything was cut short, that the hair was cut short, and that the time was no longer than from mid night to mid day."

In 1816, when she was already suffering from the dropsical ailment that was to cause her death three years later, Jemima Wilkinson went to Canandaigua to sit for her portrait. The painter was John L. D. Mathies, a skilled but self-taught artist who had opened a drawing school in Canandaigua the year before and a few years later persuaded Red Jacket to sit for a portrait—the old orator's first. In painting Jemima Wilkinson, the artist caught the personality of this remarkable sixty-four-year-old woman in an accurate likeness. Although there is no attempt to flatter, the result is not unpleasant. The strongly masculine face is intelligent; the dark eyes keen and piercing. The black hair shows no trace of gray. It is not difficult to understand how this woman could have endured the hardships of the frontier and founded and governed a religious sect. For some unknown reason, Mathies made two portraits of Jemima, one of which he never completed but kept as long as he lived. The portrait he finished for her was framed by John Malin in an elaborate frame made from the several varieties of wood that grew on the Friend's lands. It hung in her room for many years after her death.[2]

The Universal Friend's final illness was long and painful. She was visited in 1816 by Elizabeth H. Walker of West Farms, New York, who wrote detailed medical instructions to Rachel Malin.

Notwithstanding a quick succession of public engagements prevented my writing till the present time, yet the sympathetic impressions Thy trying situation produced on my mind were of the permanent nature which are not easily eradicated—Thy Friend declining, and sometimes for a long season confined, and from what I could gather when with you, not all friendly by whom you are surrounded.

I consider that discharge from her feet favorable and should be encouraged if it again suppurates. It will tend to carry off that offending matter which if not discharged must have produced agonizing pain, or if ascending the stomach prove fatal.

I apprehend an abstemious diet and as much exercise as can possible be taken will prove favorable. Let the inflamed parts of feet and legs be folded round with raw cotton made very soft by carding. Perspiration should by all means be promoted by wearing flannel next to the Boday and drinking weak warm liquids. Let a strong solution of salt petre be prepared, taking three or four times a day in a wineglass of this Nitre after which immediately drink twice the quantity of old strong cider strongly impregnated with scraped horse-radish and rolled mustard seed—this acting as a diuretic will carry off the dropsical humous by wine.

Such medication must have compounded the discomfort and pain of the dropsical condition from which Jemima suffered. (Her wooden medicine chest, full of vials and bottles containing remnants of various ill-smelling liquids, still exists.) She continued to preach, however, until her tired body could carry her no longer; "21st 11 Mo 1818 was the last time the Friend attended meeting," was written of her last regular appearance. When her sister, Patience Wilkinson Potter, died on April 19, 1819, the Friend was carried to the funeral services and preached her final public sermon. The self-assurance that characterized her forty-three-year ministry did not leave her as death approached. In spite of severe pain she continued to receive old friends and followers at her bedside, admonishing them to be faithful and demonstrating her own faith and courage.

The end came at last on July 1, 1819. Her last words, according to a family genealogy, were: "My friends I must soon depart—I am going—this night I leave you." The simple notation in the Death Book was: "25 minutes past 2 on the Clock, The Friend went from here." The next day was Saturday, the regular meeting day, and Huldah Barnes, who was present, remembered that a meeting was held as usual at the house and that the Friend's sister, Marcy Aldrich, preached. After the meeting, Huldah's aunt took her upstairs to Jemima's room, where the Friend was laid out on a special cherry board, wrapped in a winding sheet. "I remember that my Aunt said, as she lifted the covering from the face of the corpse, 'Huldah, The Friend has left us.' The countenance of The Friend had a calm and pleasant expression," she recalled many years later.

As the news of the death of the Universal Friend traveled, about a hundred people gathered about the house on the Sunday after her death, expecting a funeral service. Instead, a regular service was held, similar to the one of the day before, according to the wishes of the Friend, who wanted no display at her funeral. An oval glass window was set in the top of her coffin, and on the piece of wood cut out was inscribed, "Departed this life Universal Friend on the first day of July in the forty-third year of the Friend's testimony," together with the words of the text chosen for her funeral, from Proverbs 8:8-9: "All the words of my mouth are in righteousness; there is nothing forward or perverse in them. They are all plain to him that understandeth, and right to them that find knowledge." Four days after her death the body was placed in a vault that had been built in the cellar, with thick stone walls and a heavy plank door fastened with large spikes. There is no truth in the story that her followers kept her body unburied for several days because they expected that she would rise again.

There can be no doubt that the sixty-seven-year-old woman was prepared to meet her Maker and died confident that she would do so. William Bentley, D.D., recorded in his diary on Sunday, July 25, 1819:

We hear of the death of Jemima Wilkinson, aet. 70., [*sic*] This extraordinary woman has been the minister of a most wretched fanaticism. . . . She took leave of her friends . . . with the utmost compose & met death with the calmness of a saint & the fullness of hope. The power of religious principle when it has full hold of the mind may be seen in our country as well as in the superstitions of the east & the sacrifices of the Jugernaut.

Obituaries appeared in newspapers throughout the eastern United States, including Boston, Providence, New York, Baltimore, and Washington, D.C. In several instances the notice of her death provided an excuse to give a short account of her life and to repeat some of the stories associated with her. Charles Mowry, editor of the *American Republican*, a weekly paper published in Downington, Pennsylvania, recalled in his newspaper some of the anecdotes he heard about her when he was a child in Smithfield, Rhode Island. "These particulars are gleaned from the wreck of our earliest recollections," he confessed, "and may not be in every particular strictly correct. We hope, however, that someone will publish a detailed statement of her life and conduct. If correctly done, we have no doubt it would be interesting." Mowry recalled "an anecdote which was currently reported in her neighborhood, before she left Rhode Island."

One of her female followers, had made a very elegant piece of check. The *Friend*, being at her house, on a visit, the lady shewed the check to her, and as an evidence of devotion to her leader, proposed presenting her with a pattern off the piece for her own use. The *Friend* solemnly replied, *"The Lord hath need of the whole piece,"*—and bore it off.

The recollections of Editor Mowry were reprinted in the Washington, D.C., *National Intelligencer* and prompted a reply from "A Neighbor" in Ontario County, New York, who wrote in a letter to the editors:

I have lived for six years a neighbor, and frequently an inmate of the family of Jemima Wilkinson, and of those of her society: A wonder she certainly was! and the tongue of man has uttered every thing respecting her which folly, wonder, and malice could prompt. It would be gratifying to me, and I presume to very many others, to see a correct history of her life, ministry, and doctrines, written with intelligence and candor. But the idle and malicious tales in circulation, respecting her, are utterly unworthy of belief.

The controversy over what sort of person this woman evangelist really was continued unabated by her death.

The Publick Universal Friend made a will on the twenty-fifth of the second month, 1818, almost a year and a half before she finally "left time." Only the unpleasant experience of decades of legal controversy could have persuaded her that such a document was necessary to protect her property for the benefit of her loyal followers. This woman, who had recognized no other name than the Publick Universal Friend for more than four decades, was compelled by fear of a legal disadvantage to admit that she was the one "who in the year one thousand seven hundred and seventy six was called Jemima Wilkinson and ever since that time the Universal Friend a new name which the mouth of the Lord Hath named." All her land and property, carefully enumerated in legal style, was left to Rachel and Margaret Malin, who were entrusted with the care of the society. Her concern was for her "family" and those of her society who could not provide for themselves. She declared:

My will is that all the present members of my family and Each of them be employed if they please and if employed supported during natural life by the said Rachel and Margaret and when ever any of them becomes unable to help themselves they are according to such inability Kindly to be taken care of by the said Rachel and Margaret and my Will also is that all poor persons belonging to the society of universal Friends shall receive from the said Rachel & Margaret such assistance comfort & support during natural life as they may need and in case any either of my family or else where in the society shall turn away such shall forfeit the provision herein made for them.

The will itself was signed "The Publick universal Friend" and was witnessed by John and Ann Collins and Sarah Gregory. Evidently Thomas R. Gold, the lawyer from Whitesboro, visited Jerusalem and became concerned that the signature would be misinterpreted in the eyes of the law. A codicil further identifying the Universal Friend as Jemima Wilkinson was added on July 7, 1818, and signed with an X. This was witnessed by Gold, John Briggs, and James Brown, Jr. The fact that this resolute woman refused to sign the name Jemima Wilkinson, yet, when forced by legal necessity to make a signature, signed an X as "her cross or mark" has misled some writers to conclude that she could not read or write.

One of those present at the services on the Sunday following the death of Jemima Wilkinson remembered an interesting prophecy made by one of four Quakers who came together in a carriage from somewhere in Cayuga County. After the services, one of the four, a woman, mounted the horse block in the yard and delivered a short discourse. She compared the Universal Friend's society to a ladder or flight of steps and predicted that, now the main prop was gone, all the other props would fall out, one after another, until the whole structure disappeared. The prophecy did not require special astuteness. Actually, the society of Universal Friends had begun slow disintegration some time before the death of its leader.

The fall was not a sudden collapse, however, but rather a gradual withering away. This was due in part to the remarkable longevity of those who remained true to the teachings of the Universal Friend. Benefits from the Friend's estate were paid out for forty-three years after her death, the same length of time she had preached, and Henry Barnes, the last surviving member of the society, did not die until 1874. Rachel and Margaret Malin maintained the large house both as a home for those of the Friend's family who remained and as the headquarters of the society; and they continued to hold regular meetings for worship there. In spite of the diminution caused by litigation expenses, the Universal Friend's estate was sufficiently ample to provide comfortably not only for the dependent members of the society but also for a multitude of Malin relatives who descended upon Jerusalem soon after the death of the Universal Friend.

Nothing could better illustrate the predominance exercised by Jemima Wilkinson in the society of Universal Friends than the metamorphosis that took place in the society after her death. Although kindly and well-meaning, Rachel and Margaret Malin were utterly incapable of independent leadership. James Brown, Jr., was a good farmer and managed the business affairs of the society efficiently, but he lacked the qualities necessary to direct a religious organization. There was no lack of would-be leaders, however. Several adventurers who volunteered their services as spiritual guides and indicated their willingness to share the material resources of the society made their way to Jerusalem.

One such was a Michael H. Barton, a former Quaker from Dutchess County, who came to Jerusalem about 1830 and won the confidence of Rachel Malin and James Brown, Jr., but not that of Margaret Malin. Two others, George S. Clark and Osa Hymes, moved into the Friend's house and with Barton succeeded in adding some new features to the faith and traditions of the Universal Friend. "They claimed to give a fresh inspiration of the Friend's doctrine, but the results were a notable departure therefrom," noted Cleveland in his *History of Yates County;* "the strictness of the Friend's faith and discipline, was not maintained by the new infusion." Hymes was eventually "driven off," and Barton reluctantly moved on, but George S. Clark married a niece of the Malin sisters and remained to share in the ultimate division of the property. "After his marriage," Cleveland says, "he made little if any pretence to religious character, and his career was not favorable to the interests of the establishment or his own welfare."

Margaret Malin was the more stable of the two sisters and while she lived the property of the Universal Friend was retained and used for the support of the society as the Friend had intended. Litigation and other expenses necessitated the sale of some of the land, and over 1,700 acres were disposed of between 1828, when the last of the legal cases was decided, and the death of Margaret Malin on June 23, 1842. This land brought an average price of about eight dollars an acre and realized nearly $14,000. Margaret Malin, who was about seventy-two years old when she died, left her share of the Universal Friend's estate and property to James Brown, Jr., with the responsibility of carrying out the Friend's wish to provide for the members of her household and society.

As early as 1837, Rachel Malin showed signs of such poor judgment that a friend questioned the soundness of her mind. After death removed the protection of her sister Margaret, she became an easy victim of the persons who surrounded her and played upon her weakness to serve their selfish interests. Between 1843 and 1845 over three thousand acres of the Universal Friend's estate was distributed among sixteen of Rachel Malin's nieces and nephews or their spouses. Of the twenty-six deeds involved in the distribution, sixteen were for token considerations of one dollar, or a dollar plus "natural love and affection."

In February, 1845, after most of the valuable land in Jerusalem was already in the hands of the Malin clan, Rachel Malin established a trust to provide for the poor and needy members of the Friend's society as required by the Universal Friend's will and to carry out the terms of a bequest from William Turpin, who left $6,000 to Rachel Malin in 1833, to be used "to aid poor friends." The total assets set aside, and deeded to James Brown, Jr., and John A. Gallet as trustees, were two items: a forty-four-acre farm in Milo, then being leased for ninety-one dollars a year, to a man who had an option to buy it for $1,300; and a mortgage worth about $2,500. Brown seems to have made a sincere effort to carry out the obligations of the trust, paying out sums of money to provide care for indigent members of the society until 1862. When Rachel Malin died on January 2, 1847, the rest of the Universal Friend's property of any value was distributed among her relatives according to the terms of her will. The Friend's house went to a niece, Mary Ann Clark, the wife of George S. Clark. James Brown, Jr., and John A. Gallet were the executors of the will. From then on, Brown's Greek-revival farmhouse, a short distance southwest of the Friend's mansion, became a haven for the surviving members of the Universal Friend's society, who looked to him for assistance.

Although James Brown, Jr., was always loyal to the doctrines of the Universal Friend, he did not live out his life in obedience to her recommendation of celibacy. In 1844, at the age of sixty-seven, he married twenty-one-year-old Anna Maria Clark, a grand-niece of the Malin sisters who had grown up with them in the Friend's house. With his virility undiminished either by age or years of continence, James Brown and Anna Maria had four daughters, born between 1848 and 1856, three of whom lived to maturity. James Brown was the last recognized leader of the Universal Friends, and his death on July 30, 1863, at the age of eighty-seven marked the end of the society as an organization.

After lying for several years in the stone vault in the basement of her house, the body of Jemima Wilkinson was removed and buried in an unmarked grave by two of her followers. One of these was James Brown, Jr. The identity of the other is not known. The tradition is that the secret of her grave was handed down to the oldest child in each generation in the families of the two men who buried her. The mystery of her burial place has excited much curiosity through the years, but her preference for an unmarked grave is simply another heritage of her Quaker background. Like the early Quakers, she felt that gravestones were an unseemly vanity, and as long as she lived none were erected over the last resting places of the members of her society in either City Hill Cemetery or the Friend's Burying Ground in Jerusalem. Only in the years after her direct influence was removed did a few headstones appear.[3]

For nearly one hundred and fifty years, folks in Yates County have speculated about the place where the Friend is buried. Some persons have even tried digging to locate the spot, and a number of conflicting hypotheses about the location are in circulation. These are among the many stories about the Universal Friend, still told, not only in New York State but in the other places where she was known. Out of this body of folklore evolved an image of a folk character that almost entirely obscured the historical Jemima Wilkinson.

Chapter X

Legend and Lore

ALTHOUGH Jemima Wilkinson has received little recognition in the history of religion in America, she has
lived on in the stories that the very old delight to tell
and to which the very young only half listen. Then, when
the very young are older and the original storyteller is
gone, they wish they had paid more attention and could
remember the details. From scores of such anecdotes,
handed down from one generation to another, evolved the
folk image of Jemima Wilkinson. In Yates County, New
York, the folklore characterization of the Universal Friend,
derived from the reminiscences of her neighbors and the
descendants of her followers, usually depicted a sincere,

kindly, benevolent woman who taught basic religious and moral principles and who sought to defend the weak and poor against selfish, greedy forces. In her native New England, however, the name of Jemima Wilkinson was synonymous with fraud and delusion. The tales handed down verbally were accounts that reinforced this characterization or that tickled the Yankee appreciation of shrewdness. Most of the stories about the Friend were recorded in the century and a half after her exploits, but some of them have circulated in the oral tradition down to the present time, told by people who heard them far back in the past and never saw them written down.[1]

The legend most commonly associated with Jemima Wilkinson in every region where she is remembered is about walking on water. Like a true folk tale, it is always told in reference to a specific location, which varies, of course, with the storyteller. Sneech Pond and other bodies of water in Cumberland and Smithfield, Worden Pond in South Kingstown, Yawgoog Pond in Exeter, the Taunton River near Swansea, the Housatonic River near New Milford, the Schuylkill River near Philadelphia, and various sites on Seneca and Keuka lakes are all credited with being the exact place. The story has several variants, although not as many as locations. In the most common version, Jemima agreed to satisfy skeptics of her divine power by walking on the water like Christ. A crowd gathered at the appointed place, and Jemima appeared in her usual robes and began to preach a stirring sermon on faith, punctuated by the question, "Do ye have faith?" Finally at the end of her long exhortation she looked straight at the assembled group and asked, "Do ye have faith? Do ye believe that I can do this thing?" "We believe," chorused the crowd. "It is good," declared the prophetess, and added, as she departed with a flourish, "If ye have faith ye need no other evidence."

Another form of the tale demonstrates the same Yankee astuteness. This time the crowd was more skeptical and, when asked if they had faith, replied that they wanted proof. Again the tables were turned on them when Jemima declared, "Without thy faith I cannot do it." Still other versions have a synthetic flavor. In these Jemima is represented as actually walking on the water supported by a platform built just below the surface. Of course, someone removed several boards, and she tumbled in to the discomfort of the faithful and the delight of the skeptics.

The device of appealing to the faith of listeners is of course an old one; it is used in Arabian folk tales. The walking-on-water notion also was used by others; it became associated with Joseph Smith, of Mormon fame, and so moved west after Jemima Wilkinson's death. For many persons, however, the walking-on-the-water legend was their only identification of Jemima Wilkinson. Bertrand Russell used the tale in one of his essays, and Edwin O'Connor had Frank Skeffington recount the story in *The Last Hurrah*. Its authenticity in the Friend's case was strongly denied by Jemima's close friends and followers, who always insisted that the Universal Friend never claimed that her call to preach gave her any divine powers. It is possible, if it has any basis in fact, that it may be from a sermon in which she attempted to quiet the critics who challenged her assumption of the role of preacher by demanding that she show some sign of her divinity. Taking her text from Matthew 12:39, she discoursed in great detail on the statement, "An evil and adulterous generation seeketh after a sign," concluding with the last of her text, "and there shall no sign be given to it."

Another legend also involves miraculous powers—this one, the ability to raise the dead. If, as is entirely possible, Jemima Wilkinson prayed for a miracle by the coffin of Susannah Potter, this too may have some basis in fact, but the story itself is a typical folk-tale exaggeration. Again, according to the story, the event is staged to impress critics. One of the faithful is persuaded to feign death, and is wrapped in winding cloth and placed in a coffin. Included in the crowd, attracted by the announcement that the Universal Friend would raise this person from the dead, is an army officer, who interrupts to ask if he may plunge his sword through the corpse before the resurrection to prove that it is really dead. As he unsheathes his sword, the "corpse" springs from the coffin and dashes away, trailing his winding sheet after him. An early version of this story was recorded by the Marquis de Barbé-Marbois about 1782, but was told as pertaining to Mother Ann Lee of the Shakers.

The memory of Jemima Wilkinson still stirs a deep animosity in New England. Those left behind resented her drawing off the followers to New York State so intensely that they instilled in their descendants a bitterness about the woman that remains and can yet kindle a reaction to the name Jemima Wilkinson not unlike the response to a dirty word. Nothing was too bad to impute to her; and she was charged with blasphemy, fraud, sexual promiscuity, and even murder. One version of the story of her prediction of the death in East Greenwich alleged that she poisoned the poor Negro to make her prediction come true. Another poison story has been told in the Rose family through the years, but never before published. It was recounted long ago by a member of the family who lived at the head of North Road, not far from the site of the old Potter mansion in Kingston. Mrs. Rose, the story told, had some suspicion that Jemima was interested in her husband, and when Jemima sent her a cake she did not eat it but put it on a high shelf. One of the children got to it, ate some, and became sick (or died, in another version). When the storyteller, at least five generations from the event, was questioned if the sickness might not have been from another cause, she replied with great feeling, "I tell you that cake was poison!"

Those who had the temerity to speak back to Jemima Wilkinson were remembered as local heroes. Martin Reed of South Kingstown was remembered for his "moral courage."

When the great and presumptuous imposter, Jemima Wilkinson . . . was in her glory, he hesitated not to call her a blasphemer. On hearing of this she attired herself in her robes, went to his house with the intention of overawing and subduing him to her purposes as she had done many others. She charged him with profaning her name. Claiming to be the Son of God, she threatened that if he did not repent and humble himself, she would put forth her mighty power, and blast him and his family. He answered that he entertained no gods like her in his house, and that if she did not forthwith leave he would *turn* her out; on which she troubled him no more. Mr. Reed lived to quite an advanced age . . . eighty one.[2]

A similar story is told about Elder Silas Burrows of Groton, who permitted Jemima Wilkinson to hold a meeting in his meetinghouse and then proceeded to answer her "chapter and verse." Jemima interrupted him to demand,

"Silas Burrows, dost thou know with whom thou art contending?" "Oh yes," said he, "with Jemima Wilkinson," and continued his discussion until she left and did not return to bother him again.

A popular belief, almost as familiar as the walking-on-water legend, is the myth that Jemima appropriated the belongings of her followers with the command, "The Friend hath need of that." One version, recorded in 1909, is typical of this type of story associated with Jemima Wilkinson. John Dow was plowing in his fields when a messenger sent by Jemima came to get his sleek red oxen, with the order, "The Friend hath need of them." After surveying his half-plowed field and the good weather, John Dow supposedly replied, "Go back to the Friend and tell her that if you, or she, or the devil himself, want these oxen, you can't any of you [have] them till this corn is planted."

Another apocryphal episode in which the tables were turned on the Universal Friend supposedly took place at the time she preached to the Indians encamped at the landing by Seneca Lake. After Jemima's sermon in English, the Indian preacher Good Peter followed her with a discourse in his own language. According to the tale, when the Universal Friend asked to have his words interpreted, Good Peter objected, saying, "If she is Christ, she knows what I said."

Undoubtedly some of the stories about Jemima Wilkinson were ribald, not the sort to be written down by serious scribes, and so have been lost in time. One such is still told by old-timers in Kingston, Rhode Island. It circulated as early as 1827, and disturbed Spencer Hall, the last living member of Jemima's society in Rhode Island, who always contradicted it vehemently. A true folk tale, phrased in several ways, it describes Mrs. William Potter's apprehending the Judge in Jemima Wilkinson's private quarters. She was, according to the story, singularly unmoved by Jemima's explanation that she was simply ministering to one of her lambs. "Minister to your lambs all you want," Mrs. Potter is supposed to have retorted, "but in the future please leave my old ram alone."

A similar story cropped up in New York State. It was reported by the Duc de la Rochefoucauld-Liancourt in 1795, implicating James Parker, and by a traveler in 1811, but naming Judge Potter. In the latter version a young girl of Jemima's household reported that she saw Judge Potter come into the Friend's bedroom through the window in the night. When called to account and informed it was an angel she had seen, the child answered, she believed it was an angel, as she was told, but his coat had just such buttons on it as Judge Potter wore. La Rochefoucauld-Liancourt, a rationalist with little sympathy for religious mysticism, disliked Jemima intensely and did not hesitate to record the local gossip and to draw certain conclusions of his own. He noted that a local justice of the peace assured him that one of the girls in Jemima's household had deposed that she heard the cry of a new-born infant which Jemima's Negro woman was in the process of smothering between two mattresses, an absurdity that reveals more about the Duke's credulity than about Jemima. Observing that she was surrounded by six or seven women whom he described as "all young and handsome," he concluded, "I have little doubt, but the pious devotion of these girls is fervent enough, to submit to all the caprices of the *Allfriend*."

Prominent among the unsupported accusations against the Universal Friend was that she designated some of her subordinates with the title of prophet. Sarah Richards was supposedly named the Angel Raphael in one account and the Prophet Daniel in another. James Parker was alleged to be the Prophet Elijah, according to Thomas Morris, who added some interesting details about Parker's technique. "He would, before prophesying, wear around the lower part of his waist, a bandage or girdle, tied very tight, and when it had caused the upper part of his stomach to swell, he would pretend to be filled with prophetic visions, which he would impart to the community." Not only is the trick in this yarn a physiological absurdity but such posturing would have been quickly rejected by the members of the Universal Friend's society.

Most derogatory of all the material about Jemima Wilkinson, unrelieved by any possible merit, was David Hudson's collection of anecdotes in his biography of Jemima. Some of these stories were misconstructions, based on bits of fact, but others were complete fabrications. One such myth was the account of Jemima Wilkinson's pregnancy, resulting from a supposed love affair with a British officer. Another of Hudson's tales, often repeated, was that Jemima with one of her women followers, then living with the "Treasurer of the State of Rhode Island," a Mr._____, stole $2,000 from the Treasurer's strong box and fled with it to Worcester, Pennsylvania, in December, 1787. A messenger overtook them just as they arrived and recovered $800, which he returned to Rhode Island; there the whole incident was hushed up to protect the reputation of "two or three wealthy and respectable families." Although Hud-

son does not say so, others in retelling the story assumed
that the "Treasurer of the State of Rhode Island" was
Judge William Potter. Judge Potter never held this office,
however, and the man who did, from 1761 to at least 1792,
was a Joseph Clarke who never had any known contact
with Jemima Wilkinson.

The general outline of this story evidently circulated at
least thirty years before Hudson wrote his book and
caused the Publick Universal Friend enough discomfort
that she filed with the local authorities an affidavit covering the facts of the case. Dated the "6th day of the 12th
month," 1790, it was signed by Alice Hazard, who explained that when she began to attend the meetings of the
Universal Friend her husband, Arnold Hazard, not only
refused to support her and her children but took their
money from the home of her father, William Potter, to
his own father's home. Mrs. Hazard, being a woman of
direct action, went to her father-in-law's, found where
the money was kept, and took what she considered to
be enough for herself and her children. This she did, she
declared, "without the Advise or Consent or knowledge
of the Universal Friend or any other Person whatsoever,
Believing it to be my right, and had no thought that any
person of Sence or Goodness would trouble themselves
about the same." Alice Hazard's father-in-law was George
Hazard, a Deputy Governor (but never Treasurer) of
Rhode Island.

The derogatory stories that circulated about Jemima
Wilkinson caused her followers and their descendants to
develop a hypersensitivity about her. None was skilled
enough to attempt a defense with a pen, but whenever they

could they recorded their denial of the stories. Sometimes acquaintances of Jemima Wilkinson who were not members of her sect spoke out to contradict misleading or untrue stories. Major Benajah Mallory, a storekeeper at the Friend's Settlement but never associated with the religious community, informed historian Orasmus Turner that the old story of Jemima's promising to walk on the water was wholly false. In 1840, "D. B. W." of Auburn, New York, who said she resided in the family of the Universal Friend from 1790 to 1797, wrote a long letter to the *Christian Advocate and Journal,* a Methodist weekly, in answer to an article about Jemima Wilkinson based almost entirely upon Hudson's biography. In it she announced:

That the following charges brought against her . . . [Jemima] are not true:—1st, That she pretended to discern the secrets of the heart; 2d, To foretel future events; 3d, To heal the sick; 4th, To walk on the water; and 5th, To raise the dead; for I know that in her public discourses and private conversations she disclaimed all pretensions to miraculous gifts. That she pretended to be superhuman or immortal in any other sense than as all the redeemed of the Lord are, is also incorrect.

Others who had been acquainted or associated with the Universal Friend attempted to correct the record when they had an opportunity. But the legendary anecdotes were so much more entertaining than the actual facts that they circulated unchecked, acquiring new details as they were told and retold, sustaining the popular image of Jemima Wilkinson as a shrewd, unscrupulous impostor whose tricks won her a fleeting notoriety but whose false pretentions ultimately brought on her downfall. As recently as twenty-five years ago, a trustee of the New Milford Historical Society felt that her reputation in that vicinity was so unsavory that if a historical marker were to be erected in her memory probably it would be quickly defaced or torn down.

In western New York, historical markers designate the location of her first settlement in the Gore and her final home, which still stands in Jerusalem. After a checkered history, her last house came into the hands of its present owners, who rescued it from disintegration. Beautifully preserved, it is a memorial to the good taste and fine craftsmanship of its builders. Other material objects relating to the Universal Friend recall this colorful pioneer of the Genesee country. Her portrait, restored to original brightness, now hangs in the museum of the Yates County Historical Society in Penn Yan, and is displayed with other artifacts of the Universal Friend, including her sidesaddle and beaver hat. The famed monogrammed coach has a place of honor in the Carriage Museum of the Granger Homestead in Canandaigua.

Yet even in the Jerusalem Township she founded, the name of Jemima Wilkinson is most often mentioned in connection with one of the folk tales she and her followers deplored, usually the story of walking on the water. From time to time individuals have examined the available evidence and sought to describe the true historical figure instead of the popular folk character of the legends and myths. The refusal of the family who inherited the papers and records of the Universal Friend and her society to make them public helped to perpetuate the characterization that they deplored. Not until these documents became available after 1953 was an accurate assessment of the historical Jemima Wilkinson possible. Even now, Jemima Wilkinson probably will remain better known as a folk character than as a historical personality.

Her name also appeared in folk song. An undated broadside of sixty-eight quatrains entitled, "*A Wonderful Dream*. By Miss Jemima Wilkinson, A Sleeping Preacher," describes a journey after death past the Devil to judgment before the throne of Christ, and then an assignment to return to earth.

> And then the ever blessed Judge,
>   The lamb that once was slain,
> Said, yet you must not enter there,
>   But must return again,
>
> And live on earth from whence you came,
>   And fight the glorious fight
> Against the devil, world and sin,
>   And put them all to flight.
>
> For I will grant the grace of faith,
>   That bright immortal shield,
> And other prov'd celestial arms,
>   To aid you in the field.

Although the broadside was a sympathetic account of Jemima's vision and call to preach, it would not have borne the name Jemima Wilkinson if it had been authorized by her. It seems to indicate that there was enough popular interest in Jemima and her activities to make the writing and publishing of such a poem or song commercially profitable.

Her name appeared again in an 1830 song deriding the

feminist, Frances Wright. Sung to the tune of "Oh, Put the Onion to Your Eye," the song declared,

> She beat Jemima Wilkinson
> Joana Southcote quite,
> E'en mother Lee was nothing to
> Our little Fanny Wright.

Jemima Wilkinson's companions in this little verse indicate the kind of woman with whom her memory was associated in the public mind. Joanna Southcott, an English mystic who began to prophesy in 1792, was better known than Jemima because of numerous publications of her memoirs, prophecies, letters, and verses by some of her more literate apostles. Mother Ann Lee was more original than Jemima, and the society of Shakers was more enduring than that of the Universal Friend, although, again, much of the credit for the survival is due to the successors of Ann Lee. Jemima Wilkinson had none of the wit and intellect of Fanny Wright and would have been shocked beyond measure by some of Fanny's ideas, but she did make easier the role of Fanny Wright and other women who sought to break out of their traditional position. Jemima was the only one of the four who was a native-born American; no other American woman equaled her achievements as a religious leader until the advent of Mary Baker Eddy.

Contrary to the impression created by the legends and folklore, Jemima Wilkinson undoubtedly was sincere in her belief that her call to preach was divinely inspired. Although she was handicapped by an inadequate education and a limited breadth of experience, her religious fanaticism, combined with such natural attributes as a dynamic personality, a sense of the dramatic, and effective speaking ability, made her a highly successful evangelical preacher. To the chagrin of some men, she demonstrated that a woman could stand before large crowds and preach a sermon that many found moving. She was accepted as a leader of both men and women and inspired one of the earliest settlements in western New York. Few women of the colonial period of American history have matched the accomplishments of Jemima Wilkinson, the Publick Universal Friend.

Appendix I

Death Book of the Society

of Universal Friends

Jerusalem 28th of the 10th m° 1794—
By living witnesses of the deceased, I have the following History, until the Year 1785. From which Time untill the present My own Personal Acquaintance has inform'd Me, being an Eye & an Ear Witness of the departure of my Friends:

RUTH PRICHARD.

––––

Fear Hathaway, Daughter of N. and Freelove H: Left time 13th of the 5th M° 1773 22 Years of age: She found peace & Satisfaction in her last sickness; Speak of the distruction that was coming on the world: And She said the Lord is coming; and He will come still

Ruth Spencer dyed on the morning of the 21 of March 1819 in the full belief of the Public Universal Friend. She was sudnly snached out of Time She was seised with a fit of the Palsy and Expired in less than one Minute. [This entry written in another hand]

Susannah Potter, left Time 19th of the 5th M° 1780. 22 Years of Age. She died in the Arms of the Friend.

Mary Hathaway, left Time 6th of the 4th M° 1782: She left a lively Testamony of the great Day of Visitation, that has come in this our Day. She went away Rejoicing; 43 Years of Age.

Elizabeth Parker left Time

Abigail Holm's left Time 20th of the 4th M° 1782:

Abraham Richards, left Time 25th of the 3d M° 1786: Aged

Cloe Keeny, left Time 7th of the 5th M° 1786; Aged 22

Elizabeth Rose, left Time 2d of the 3d M° 1787: Aged 6 Years, She was a wonderful Child; whome the Friend loved.—

Hannah Porter, left Time 16th of the 6th M° 1787: Aged

Merrida Mallery left Time

Rhoda Sherman, left Time

Rhoda Wescot, left Time

Elizabeth Holmes left Time 18th of the 2 M° 1789:

Epharim Keeny, left Time, 9th of the 10th M° 1789:

Huldah Andress left Time, 17th of the 11th M° 1789: Aged

Lucy Holmes, left Time, 11th of the 8th M° 1790: She found the Lamb of God. Believing in the Day of her Visitation. She went away rejoicing; giving glory to God and the Lamb. This departed Saint, as the avenues of mortal life were closing, lifted up her hands in Prayer, said Glory to God in the highest, and unto the Lamb, forever and ever! Saying (with an emphasis which no mortal language can describe) Looking at the Friend, My dear Redeemer; I love; I love; I love; She was

William Aldrich, in His journeying to this New Settlement, Sicken'd and Died. He was aged 35. Went away into the world of Spirits rejoicing, 18th of the 5th M° 1791: His dying Testimony was not then written: But this He said, The Universal Friend, was a Messenger sent from God.

Candace Kenny, Left Time, 19th of the 3^{d} M° 1791. Aged 15^{n}. She in Her last moments, Called out My Friend! My Friend! And while The Friend was Praying, She departed: And left an evidence of Faith unfained.—

Anna Brown, left Time, 16th of the 4th M° 1791: Aged   She gave her Children to the Friend, desireing them to mind the Friend; She called to those around her to come and see Death! Lifting up her hands, says Read This. After which, She expir'd, And it appears, went Home in peace, Where weary Souls find reast.

The aged Jonathon Botsford, Left Time, 20th of the 4th M° 1791: He was aged about 80 years.

Asa Richards,

Lavina Briggs, left time 2^{d} of the 10 M° 1791: Leaving a Satisfactory evidence of a happy Change. She was aged 56: She told the friends to hold the beginning of their Confidence steadfast unto the end.—

Jacob Weaver, an Ethiopian, left time

John Bartleson, left time 2^{d} of the 12 M° 1785: Aged 26.

Peleg Wood, left time

William Potters Negro Boy, Cuff, left time   The Friends Text upon this Occasion was, Because there is Wrath beware; lest He also take Thee away. &c

John Briggs, left time

Esther Briggs, left time

Anna Prosser, left time

Asa Richards, left time 27 of the 6th M° 1792: He search'd
after iniquity 'till he could find none: The Friend attended
him in his last moments; whome he looked upon when bath'd
with the cold sweat of Death, and said he had a comfortable
Hope. He was buryed on the 29. The Friend's Text was in
Prov. The wicked is driven away in his wickedness but the
Righteous hath hope in his Death.—

Mehitabil Smith, left Time 10th of the 3^d M° 1793: After about
3 Months illness, She gladly resigned her Breath Saying in her
last moments, O! How I love my Lord; He is all and in all
to my Soul: Glory to God and the Lamb. On the 13th The
Corpse was decently buried   The Dear Friend attended the
Funeral, held Meeting at the House   The Text was Isaiah
57th Chapt. 1st, 2^d, verses, The Righteous perisheth and no
Man layeth it to heart; and merciful men are taken away, none
considering that the Righteous is taken away from the evil to
come. He shall enter into peace, they shall rest in their beads;
each one walking in his uprightness. — At the grave, Friend
said, This is the end of all men; and the living will lay it to
heart. They that obey are the living. Before the burying I
heard the Friend by the Corps repeat this,

> The eyes that Seldom could close,
> With Sorrows forbiden to sleep;
> Seald up in eternal repose,
> Have strangely forgotten to weep!

And the Friend Said Precious in the Sight of the Lord is the
Death of his Saints. — She was aged 46.

Anna Jones left time, 16th of the 8 M° 1793.

Eunice Manswer Departed this life 13th of the 9th M° 1793: It appeared She was prepared in a short time to fulfill a long time: The Friend attended the Funeral, Text was

Jerusha Ingriham left time 16th of the 9th M° 1793: Leaving an evidence of a happy Change; She said Prepare to meet the Great I — AM! The Friend attended Her funeral, Had a great Meeting; Text was This, Who is a God like unto Thee, that pardoneth eniquity, and passeth by the transgressions of the remnants of thy People

Sarah Friend or Sarah Richards, left time 30th, and last of the 11th M° 1793. Seventh Day of the Week which is the Sabath, at Eve 7n on the clock She Expired! And left Her weeping friends to mourn for themselves! Seventeen weeks She patiently endur'd one fever after another, till at last — These scenes of grief and Sorrows inexprest; Did waft her soul to everlasting Rest! 4th of the 12 M°. The Friend attended Her Funeral, and Preach'd a very great Sermon. The exortation began thus, It is better to go to the house of mourning than to the house of feasting, for that is the end of all men, and the living will lay it to heart; And the Text was, The Righteous perisheth, and no man layeth it to heart; and merciful men are taken away, none considering that the Righteous is taken away from the evil to come; They shall enter into peace, They shall rest in their beds, each one walking in his uprightness. She was aged 36.

Armenia Potter left time 15th of the 2d M° of 1794. The Friend was with her in her last moments, and had Satisfaction in her death; 18th, The dear Friend attended Her funeral, held Meeting at Holmes's, Text was in Micha VII. 18. Who is a God like unto Thee, that pardoneth iniquity, and passeth by the transgressions of the remnant of his heritage; For He retaineth not His Anger forever because He delighted in Mercy. She was aged 2 [?]

Euni[c]e Kenny left time 27th of 4th M° 1794: She said I shall be happy; I shall be happy! The Friend was with Her at the last; She wished for the last moment to come! That she might reach her celestial home. The Corpse was brought to the Meeting. The Friends Text was in Psalms   Blessed is the people that know the joyful sound   A great sermon this Day; after which The dear Friend attended the burying of the Corpse which was decently laid in the silent earth—

Elisha Ingraham left time

James Hathaway left time 16th of the 12th M° 1790. He was aged

Thomas Hathaway left time 25th of the 8th M° 1795: Aged

Lydia Coggsal, left Time 7th of the 7th M° 1796: She was aged 56.

Amos Gearnsey seign. left time 7th of the 9th M° 1796: Aged 65. He went down to the silent Mansions in peace; The Friend closed his Eyes; attended the funeral; Preach'd a Sermon from Hebrews 9. 27. 28. An as it is appointed unto Men once to die, and—

Samuel Botsford, A young Man in the bloom of life, was suddenly struck out of time by the fall of a Tree. His age 20 years & 5 Months, lacking 2 Days:

The Aged Benjamin Brown left Time first Day of the Year 1797: First of the   M° and 1st of the W. Calm & Serene was the close of life. His Age was

The Aged Freelove Hathaway left Time

Lydia Hunt was suddenly snatch'd out of Time, perhaps one hours warning; and then a disembody'd Spirit!—The Friend attended the Solemnity of the funeral and Preach'd from these words   Watch Ye! Therefore; For Ye Know not what hour your Lord doth Come!

Abigail Botsford, left Time 22 of the 2ᵈ Mᵒ 1797: Aged 52:—

David Waggoner left time

Lucy Botsford left time

Margaret Briggs left Time 6ᵗʰ of the 7ᵗʰ Mᵒ 1800   Her life being an example of steadfast piety and uprightness, She meet death with joy and went down to the grave in Peace. being 66 Years of Age.

Jedidiah Holmes Junr left Time

Mary Sherord left Time

Francis Brown left Time

Benaijah Botsford, By a Sudden Stroke was called out of Time

The Aged Elizabeth Botsford left time last day of the 10 Mᵒ Aged 87. She was more that willing to Die—

Elizabeth Ovett, Left Time

Sarah Renyolds, Departed this life 12 of the 4ᵗʰ Mᵒ 1803. Aged 48 years.

Adam Hunt departed this life 12 of the 4ᵗʰ Mᵒ 1803: Aged 69. He was desireous to depart, and to be with his Lord.

Peleg Briggs Departed this life 19ᵗʰ 5ᵗʰ Mᵒ 1807: being 78 years of age:—

William Wall departed this life 30ᵗʰ of the 1ˢᵗ Mᵒ 1803: at half past 12, On the Clock P.M. His Age

Mary Dains, Departed this life 15ᵗʰ of the 6 Mᵒ

Mehetabil Botsford left time

Mary Botsford, suddenly depart this life, Supposed to be poisond

Sarah Coggsal left time

Huldah Botsford left time

Anna Prosser left time

Yong Elizabeth Holmes left time 23^d of the 9th M° 1810. Aged 35—

Bethany Sisson Left our dark Hemisphere, we hope to shine in a higher & brighter Orb: She departed this life

Elizabeth Kinyon left time 18th of the 12 M° 18 [?]

Amos Gearnsey left time the 10th of the 9 M° AD 1814 the 7 day of the Week, at 8 on the Clock in the Morn. Agd

Jedidiah Holmes Seni. left time the 2[?] of the 5th M° AD 1814. The third day of the Week, His age

John Renyolds left time 2[?] of the 7 M° 1814. aged

Margt Hunt left time

Elizabeth Keeny left time 18 of the 12 M° 1816. Aged

Solomon Ingraham was suddenly snatch out of time 16th of the 12 M° 1815: 7 day of the Week, about the time he should have dresst for Meeting: he was buried alive in the bottome of the Pitt which he help'd to dig.—

Caty White was ill but a few hours, and then expir'd 28 of the [?] M° 1817, aged

Elizabeth Durham

Abel Botsford left time 17th of the 8 M° 1817: aged all most 70 years. All his children left time before him, So that it made good the prediction, "That this Man shall die Childless."—

Jacob Wagoner left time 26th of the 5th M° AD 1818, aged 67 years:—

Susanah Wagoner left time 30 of the 8 M° 1818 — Aged 67 years.

[End of Ruth Prichard Spencer's handwriting. Entries continued in another hand.]

Stephen Luther left time the 17th of the 2 M° 1829 — in the 28 years of his Age

Elijah Botsford left time the 1 of the 5 M° 1829—Aged

Mary Holmes left time the 21 of the 9 M° 1829.

Isaac Nicholls left time the 23 of the 12 M° 1829.

Silas Spink left time the 9 of the 10 M° 1830

Hannah Hunt left time the 20 of the 10 M° 1830

Nathanael Ingraham left time the 26 of the 2 M° 1831 in the 83 year of this Age

Mary Botsford left time the 31 of the 3 M° 1831 in the 81 year of her age.

Elizabeth Botsford left time the 12 of the 4 [or 7] M° 1830.

[Front Cover]

4th of the 4th M° 1797 Sabath Day I had the Solemn news of my Fathers Death! — Since contradicted:—

25 minutes past 2 on the Clock, The Friend went from here.—

Appendix II

The Universal Friend's Advice, to Those of the Same Religious Society.

RECOMMENDED TO BE READ IN THEIR PUBLIC MEETINGS FOR DIVINE WORSHIP.

THE PUBLIC UNIVERSAL FRIEND

ADVISETH all, who desire to be *one* with the *Friend* in spirit, and to be wise unto salvation, that they be punctual in attending meetings, as many as conveniently can.

That they meet at the *tenth hour* of the day, as near as possible.

That those, who cannot well go to meetings, sit down at

their several homes, about the time meeting begins, in order to wait for and upon the LORD.

That they shun, at all times, the company and conversation of the wicked *world,* as much as possible: But when any of you are under a necessity of being with them, do your business with few words, and retire from them as soon as you can get your business done; remembering to keep on your watch, and pray for assistance, especially when the *wicked* are before you.

That you do not enquire after news, or the public reports of any one; and be careful not to spread any *yourselves,* that are not of the LORD.

That you deal justly with all men, and do unto all men as you would be willing they should do unto you; and walk orderly, that none occasion of stumbling be given by you, to any.

Let all your conversation, at all times, be such as becometh the gospel of CHRIST.

Do good to all as opportunity offers, especially to the *household of faith.*

Live peaceably with all men as much as possible; in an especial manner do not strive against one another for mastery, but all of you keep your ranks in righteousness, and let not one thrust another.

Let not debate, evil surmisings, jealousies, evil speaking, or hard thinking be named among you; but be at peace among yourselves.

Take up your daily cross against all ungodliness and worldly lusts; and live as you would be willing to die, loving one another, forgiving one another, as ye desire to be forgiven by GOD and his HOLY ONE.

Obey and practice the devine counsel you have heard, or may hear from time to time; living every day as if it were the *last;* remembering you are always in the presence of the HIGH and LOFTY ONE who inhabiteth eternity, whose name is HOLY; and, without holiness, no one can see the LORD in peace, therefore, be ye holy in all your conversation, and labor to keep yourselves unspotted from the world, and possess your vessels in sanctification and honor, knowing, that ye ought to be temples for the HOLY SPIRIT to dwell in; and, if your vessels are unclean, that which is holy cannot dwell in you: And know ye not your ownselves, that if CHRIST dwells not, yea, and reigns not in you, ye are in a reprobate state, or out of favor with GOD and his HOLY ONE; therefore, ye are to shun the very appearance of evil in all things, as foolish talking, and vain jesting, with all unprofitable conversation, which is not convenient, but flee from bad company as from a serpent. Be not drunk with wine, or any other spirituous liquors, wherein is excess; but be filled with the HOLY SPIRIT, building one another up in the most holy faith, praying in the HOLY GHOST.

Keep yourselves in the love of GOD, and when you come into *Meetings* or *Evening Sittings,* make as little stir as possible, that you may not disturb the solemn meditations of others, but consider you are drawing near to approach the holy, pure, eternal SPIRIT, that cannot look on sin with any allowance.

Endeavour to meet all at one time, and keep your seats until meeting is over, except upon some extraordinary occasion.

Gather in all your wandering thoughts, that you may sit down in solemn silence, to wait for the aid and assistance of the HOLY SPIRIT, and not speak out vocally in meetings, except ye are moved thereunto by the HOLY SPIRIT, or that there be a real necessity. Worship GOD and His HOLY ONE in spirit and in truth.

Use plainness of speech and apparel, and let your adorning, not be outward, but inward, even that of a meek and quiet spirit, which, in the sight of GOD is of great price. Thus saith the Psalmist—It is most like the King's daughter, all glorious within; her clothing is of wrought gold.

Consider how great a thing it is to worship GOD and the
LAMB acceptably, who is a Spirit, and must be worshiped in
spirit and in truth: Therefore, deceive not yourselves, by in-
dulging drowsiness, or other mockery, instead of worshipping
GOD and the LAMB. GOD is not mocked, for such as each
of you sow, the same must ye also reap: If ye sow to the flesh,
ye must, of the flesh, reap corruption; but if ye are so wise
as to sow to the Spirit, ye will of the Spirit, reap life everlasting, Rom. viii. from the 6th to the 19th verse. "For to be car-
nally minded is death, but to be spiritually minded is life and
peace: Because the carnal mind is emnity against GOD; for it
is not subject to the law of GOD, neither indeed can be. So
then, they that are in the flesh cannot please GOD: But ye are
not in the flesh but in the SPIRIT, if so be that the SPIRIT of
GOD dwell in you. Now, if any man hath not the SPIRIT of
CHRIST he is none of his. And, if CHRIST be in you, the
body is dead, because of sin; but the spirit is life because of
righteousness: But if the SPIRIT of Him that raised up JESUS
from the dead dwell in you, He that raised up CHRIST
from the dead, shall also quicken your mortal bodies, by his
SPIRIT that dwelleth in you. Therefore, brethren, we are
debtors, not to the flesh, to live after the flesh. For if ye live
after the flesh, ye shall die; but if ye, through the SPIRIT do
mortify the deeds of the body ye shall live. For as many as
are led by the SPIRIT of GOD, they are the sons of GOD.
For, ye have not received the spirit of bondage again to fear;
but ye have received the SPIRIT of Adoption, whereby we
cry, *Abba, Father,* The SPIRIT itself beareth witness with our
spirits that we are the children of GOD; and, if children, then
heirs of GOD, and joint-heirs with CHRIST; If so be that we
suffer with him, that we may be also glorified together with
him. For I reckon, that the sufferings of this present time are
not worthy to be compared with the glory that shall be revealed in us." Ye cannot be my friends, except ye do whatso-

ever I command you: Therefore be not weary in well-doing, for, in due season, ye shall reap if ye faint not.

Those whose mouths have been opened to speak, or to pray in public, are to wait for the movings of the HOLY SPIRIT, and then, speak or pray as the SPIRIT giveth utterance; not running without divine authority; nor speak nor pray any longer than the SPIRIT remaineth with you; nor linger when moved to speak as mouth for the HOLY ONE, or moved to pray by the same power.

Let not contention, confusion, jarring, or wrong speaking have any place amongst you. Use not whisperings in meetings, for whisperers separate chief friends.

Above all, give all dilligence to make your calling and election sure, and work out your salvation with fear and trembling, redeeming your time, because the days are evil. Forget the things that are behind, and press forward towards the mark and the prize of the high calling of GOD in CHRIST JESUS; that ye may be found without spot or rebuke before the LORD; that ye may be delivered from the bondage of corruption, and brought into the glorious liberty of the Sons of GOD, where the Morning Stars sing together, and all the Sons of GOD shout for joy; having oil in your vessels with your lamps, like the wise virgins, trimmed and burning; having on your wedding garments, that when the HOLY ONE ceaseth to intercede for a dying world, you may also appear with him in glory, not having on your righteousness, but the righteousness of GOD in CHRIST JESUS.

You, who are PARENTS, or intrusted with the tuition of children, consider your calling, and the charge committed unto you, and be careful to bring them up in the nurture and admonition of the LORD, and educate them in a just and reverend regard thereunto: And whilst you are careful to provide for the support of their bodies, do not neglect the welfare of their souls, seeing, the earliest impression, in general, lasts the longest. As it is written, "Train up a child in the way that he should go, and when he is old, he will not, easily, depart from it;" and let example teach as loud as your precepts.

CHILDREN, obey your parents in all things, in the LORD, for it is right and acceptable in the sight of GOD. Honor your fathers and mothers, and the way to honor father and mother is not to give them flattering titles, or vain compliments, but to obey the counsel of the LORD, and them, in the LORD. Thus saith the wisdom of the LORD, by the mouth of the wise king Solomon, My son, forget not my law, but let thine heart keep my commandments, for length of days, long life, and peace, shall they add to thee. Let not mercy and truth forsake thee, bind them about thy neck, write them upon the table of thine heart, so shalt thou find favor and good understanding in the sight of GOD and man. Trust in the LORD with all thine heart, and lean not to thine own understanding; In all thy ways acknowledge Him, and He shall direct thy paths. Be not wise in thine own eyes; fear the LORD, and depart from evil. Hear, ye children, the instruction of your father, and attend to know understanding; for I give you good doctrine, forsake ye not my law. The fear of the LORD is the beginning of knowledge, but fools despise wisdom and instruction. My son, hear the instruction of thy father, and forsake not the law of thy mother, for they shall be an ornament of grace unto thy head, and chains about thy neck. My son, if sinners entice thee, consent thou not; if they say, Come, let us lay wait for blood; let us lurk privily for the innocent without cause; let us swallow them up alive as the grave, and whole as those that go down unto the pit, we shall find all precious substance, we shall fill our houses with spoil: Cast in thy lot amongst us, let us all have one purse: My son, walk not thus in the way with them; refrain thy foot from their path; for their feet run to do evil, and they make haste to shed blood. They lay in wait for their own blood; they lurk privily for their own lives; so is every one that is greedy of gain, that taketh away the life of the owners thereof. All of you be careful not to grieve away the HOLY SPIRIT that is striving with you, in this the day of your visitation, and is setting in order before you, your sins and short comings: But, turn ye at the reproofs of instruction, which is the *way* to *life.*

MASTERS, give unto your servants that which is lawful and right, and deal with other people's children, as you would be willing others should deal with you, and your children also, in your absence, knowing, that whatsoever ye would that others do unto you, ye ought to do likewise unto them; for this is the law and the prophets.

SERVANTS, be obedient to your masters according to the flesh, in fear and trembling, in singleness of heart, as unto CHRIST, doing the will of GOD from the heart, with good will doing service, as unto the LORD, and not unto man; knowing, that whatsoever good thing any man doeth, the same shall he receive of the LORD, whether he be bond or free. And you, *masters,* do the same things unto them, forbearing threatening, knowing that your Master is in heaven; neither is there respect of persons with him, but he is merciful and kind even to the unthankful and to the evil.

AND *all of you,* who have been, or may be so divinely favored, as to be, mouth for the HOLY ONE, I entreat you, in the bonds of love, that when you are moved upon to speak in public, that ye speak as the *Oracles of God,* and as the HOLY SPIRIT giveth utterance, not withholding more than it meet, which tendeth to poverty; neither add to his words, lest he reprove thee, and thou be found a liar: But do all with a single eye to the glory of GOD, that GOD and the LAMB may be glorified by you and through you; for he that winneth souls is wise, and the wise shall shine as the brightness of the firmament, and they that turn many be righteousness, as the stars for ever and ever.

THE *time is fulfilled*—the *kingdom of* GOD *is at hand.* *Repent ye*, and *believe the Gospel*, that the kingdom of GOD may begin within you.

HE hath shewed thee, O *Man!* what is good: and what doth the LORD require of thee, but to
> DO JUSTLY,
> LOVE MERCY, and
> WALK HUMBLY WITH THY GOD!
>   AMEN.

Notes

Chapter 1

1. Although it is impossible to make a positive identification of Amey Whipple Wilkinson, she could be the Amey, born on October 24, 1718, who was one of the seventeen children of William and Elizabeth (Sprague) Whipple of Smithfield. This William Whipple lived on a farm in Smithfield, not far from Lime Rock on the road from Providence to Worcester. Seven of the twelve children of Amey Wilkinson were given the same names as children of William and Elizabeth Whipple. The sources who list her as the Amey who was a daughter of Jeremiah and Deborah (Bucklin) Whipple of Attleboro are certainly wrong. This Amey died of a scald at the age of three in 1721, as her tombstone records. The Whipples were indeed a prolific family. The Rhode Island census of 1774 listed twenty-two families of Whipples in the towns of Cumberland and Smithfield alone. Amey may have been the second wife of Jeremiah, for the town records of Smithfield note the marriage of a Jememiah Wilkinson and Patience Hyde on July 3, 1735, by a justice of the peace.

2. Built in 1703, the Smithfield meetinghouse is still standing on Great Road in the village of Saylesville and is still used for regular Quaker worship. Beside it is a cemetery in which the unidentified

graves are marked only with plain field stones in accord with early Quaker practice.

3. Jeremiah Wilkinson evidently became convinced that Jemima's strange conduct was more than a temporary disturbance and he gave up accompanying her. When she left home (about 1778), he lost touch with her and eventually was reinstated as a member of the Society of Friends. He died in Cumberland on March 23, 1792. The most distinguished member of the family in Rhode Island was Jeremiah, Jr. (1741-1831), a noted inventor, who was the first to make cut nails and who invented a machine to draw wire by horsepower. He lived on Cherry Hill in Cumberland and was a Quaker in good standing all his life.

Chapter III

1. David Hudson, in his hostile biography, uses this episode to suggest a love affair with a British officer, an anonymous Major ———, who promised to resign his commission and retire to his estates in England to wait for Jemima to join him. According to Hudson, the ship to take her to England was waiting favorable winds late in June (1780), after the British evacuation of Newport, when by chance she read in a newspaper an account of a battle in which her lover was wounded. This led her to abandon her journey. The result of this affair with Major ——— was a pregnancy, Hudson insinuated, which caused Jemima to seclude herself for seven months, shortly after giving up her proposed trip to England. This, perhaps, is the most fantastic of the ridiculous stories used by Hudson, but, unlike some of the others, it destroys itself with its own details. The British fleet evacuated Newport in October, 1779. Any pregnancy involving a British officer would have been obvious long before June of the following year. Aside from the fact that sexual promiscuity seems incompatible with Jemima's messianic megalomania, it is certain that she established her headquarters in the Potter mansion in Little Rest several months before the British left Newport.

2. When the annual May session of the Rhode Island General Assembly met in 1779, the various state officers were elected as usual. Judges of the Courts of Common Pleas for each county were elected at this time with the single exception of King's County, the court

over which Judge Potter had presided since 1768. All five positions
on that court remained vacant until the next session of the General
Assembly, which met in Little Rest on June 14. Four days later, when
the members of the court were announced, Stephen Babcock was
Chief Justice, the other members of the court were re-elected, and
William Potter's name did not appear anywhere. At the same time
he ceased to be the Town Clerk of South Kingstown, an office he had
held with a few interruptions since 1752. With unusual formality, it
was voted at town meeting on June 1, 1779, to appoint a committee
"to Receive from Wilm. Potter Esqr. Late Town Clerk all the
Records Files or papers and other things belonging to said office."
Unaccountably, however, at a town meeting a month later, William
Potter, Esquire, and Captain James Parker, another follower of
Jemima Wilkinson, were appointed to a seven-member committee
of correspondence to "address and correspond" with other towns
and similar committees in other states about the "alarming State of
the Publick Currency." Judge William Potter was an important
political figure in the new state government as he had been in the
colonial government. His loyalty to the cause of independence was
never questioned. He served the revolutionary cause by apprehending and sending to the governor a man suspected of planning to join
the British in Newport, and, later, was appointed by the Council of
War to act on a committee to investigate some sequestered property. Contrary to tradition, Judge Potter was never Treasurer of
Rhode Island, nor did Joseph Clarke, who was Treasurer from 1761
to about 1792, ever have any association with Jemima Wilkinson.

3. Sarah Negus, incorrectly listed in Cleveland's *History and
Directory of Yates County* (I, 99) as Sarah Negers, was probably a
Negro herself. The Universal Friend's society had no color bar.
Chloe Towerhill, a former slave, was both a member of the society
and the Universal Friend's cook. The Death Book of the society,
recording the deaths of those who were in good standing, included
the name of William Potter's Negro boy, Cuff, and Jacob Weaver,
"an Ethiopian."

4. Some of these stories will be retold in Chapter X, "Legends and
Lore." Wilkins Updike in his *History of the Episcopal Church, in
Narragansett, Rhode Island*, published in 1847, wrote that when the

Potter homestead was finally sold to Elisha R. Potter in 1808 "the homestead, the elegant garden with parterres, borders, shrubbery, summer-house, fruit orchard—his ancient mansion, with the high costly fences, outhouses, and cookery establishment, and the more recent erections for the accommodation . . . [of Jemima Wilkinson] —were in ruins, and, within a few years, the whole buildings have been removed, and a small and suitable house for a tenant has been built in its place." J. Hagadorn Wells, who was born in Kingston (Little Rest) in 1817, recalled in his reminiscences, recorded in 1897: "There were some relics of the former gardens of the old Abbey in my early days; and more than once I joined a raiding party of young fellows, to ransack the empty apartments, scare up the ghosts of generations of rural gentry and Wilkinsonian saints, dead; but never omitting a less romantic visit to the pear trees." Wells thought that another building used as a meetinghouse was built for the Universal Friend in South Kingstown but he did not know its location. He must have been thinking of the meetinghouse in East Greenwich.

5. Professor Samuel Williams of Harvard investigated the Dark Day and believed that it was caused by a combination of smoke and a curious condition of the atmosphere, in which low-hanging clouds caught the smoke from fires burning over vast acres to clear land in New Hampshire and Vermont (*Annals of the American Academy of Arts and Sciences*, I [1785], 234-246).

6. James Parker was born June 2, 1743, one of eight children of George and Catherine Parker, who came from London and settled on a 1,200-acre plantation in West Greenwich, Rhode Island. He owned a farm in South Kingstown and in 1774 had nine members in his household, including one Negro slave. Although James had a brother, Peter, he was not the Sir Peter Parker, Admiral of the British Navy, as claimed in Cleveland's history.

7. John Rose (1742-1827) and Orpha (Sweet) Rose were members of the society of Universal Friends who did not emigrate to New York State. Much of the property of the Rhode Island followers was left in his hands to sell when he could get a good price in sound currency.

8. John and Mary Nichols gave one acre of land for a meeting-

house in East Greenwich on September 22, 1783 (Land Evidence 10:8). On June 6, 1784, William Potter bought ten acres of land in East Greenwich (Land Evidence 10:41), of which he sold two acres for a meetinghouse on September 9, 1784 (Land Evidence, 10:45). The meetinghouse was still standing in the 1820's.

9. This story was recalled by Spencer Hall, who claimed to be present when the incident took place. The house is still standing off Division Street in East Greenwich.

Chapter IV

1. Smith's statement against slavery is quoted in Rufus M. Jones, *The Quakers in the American Colonies* (London, 1911), p. 159. He wrote, "The matter was Set befor me in a Clear manner more clear than what mortal man Could have Done and theirfore I believe it is not write for me to Shirk or hide in a thing of So Greate a Consarnment as to Give my Consent to do to others Contrary to what we our Selves would be willing to be don unto." The Golden Rule, repeated so often by Jemima Wilkinson, was the reason Smith cited for his action.

2. The building was used until the Universal Friends in the New Milford area moved to New York State. In 1793 it was rented to the Episcopalian Society of New Preston, and was sold to them in 1796. It was used as an Episcopal church until the present St. Andrew's Episcopal Church in Marbledale was occupied in 1823.

3. Valentine Rathbun's first edition, printed in Providence in 1781, was entitled *An Account of the Matter, Form, and Manner of a New and Strange Religion*. . . . In this edition the name Jemima Wilkinson is inserted parenthetically after the reference in the Introduction to the woman from Rhode Island. In later editions the name in parentheses was omitted. Editions were printed in Hartford, Boston, and Norwich in 1781, and in Worcester, Boston, and Salem in 1782, and in New York in 1783.

Chapter V

1. *The American Museum* (Philadelphia), I (1787), 221.

2. The pamphlet was reprinted in Penn Yan, New York, in 1821

and in 1833. No copies of the 1784 edition have been located. The complete text is given in Cleveland's *History of Yates County*, I, 101-107. Charles Lowell Marlin includes a careful analysis of the pamphlet in an unpublished master's thesis at Indiana University (June, 1961), "The Preaching of Jemima Wilkinson." He noted, "The *Advice*, at first reading, is misleading because it appears to have no pattern or organization, yet it does have a pattern based on intuitive feelings and experience, and a persuasively sound organization completely alien to any advice she might have received and to most expositions she might have read." Marlin, who was working in the Department of Speech and Theatre, discovered in the *Advice* "a five part organization: opening, first counterpoint, body, second counterpoint, and conclusion. These terms designate divisions in the sermon characterized by two features: first, a change in subject matter or attitude; second, a change in psychological purpose." He concludes, "Clumsy, rough, and unpolished as her *Advice* may be, it still shows her insight into the psychology of communication and explains in part why she held power and influence as a religious leader during a time of highly competitive missionary work." The text of the 1833 edition is given in Appendix II.

Chapter VI

1. No official list of the names of the members of the first party of twenty-five pioneers has been found. Nineteen names are found in correspondence between James Parker and the Universal Friend and in Cleveland's *History of Yates County*. They are Gideon Aldrich, Augustus Barber, Abel Botsford, Elnathan Botsford, Jr., John Briggs, Peleg Briggs, Benjamin Brown, Sr., Stephen Card, Thomas Hathaway, Sr., Jedidiah Holmes, Sheffield Luther, Isaac Nichols, James Parker, John Reynolds, Ezekial Shearman, Thomas Sherman, George Sisson, Asahel Stone, Jacob Wagener. Six more persons arrived after the first party but before September, 1788. They are Abigail Brown, Sarah Brown, Elizabeth Holmes, Enoch Malin, William Potter, Richard Smith.

2. The seventeen members of the community who received land in the Gore were Mary Bartleson, Abel Botsford, Benjamin Brown, Sr., Benjamin Brown, Jr., Peleg Briggs, Stephen Card, Amos Garn-

sey (Guernsey), Thomas Hathaway, John Lawrence, Isaac Nichols, James Parker, William Potter, John Reynolds, Benedict Robinson, Ezekial Shearman, Hazard Sherman, and George Sisson. Eight persons who participated in one or more of the meetings to distribute the land but failed to receive a share were Marcy Aldrich, Jonathan Botsford, Jedidiah Holmes, Adam Hunt, Silas Hunt, Richard Smith, Asahel Stone, and Anna Wagener. Although the Universal Friends did not believe in taking disputes among themselves to court, some of the members who were forced off their land began legal action. In the case of Jackson, *ex. dem.* Potter and others, *v.* Sisson (Johnson, *Reports of Cases,* II, 321), Chancellor James Kent decided, on appeal in 1801, that the only legal estate created by the land grant patent was vested in the three patentees, Parker, Potter, and Hathaway. The vested interests of the associates of the community of Universal Friends was too vague to be decided in a court of law, but might be determined by an action in equity. According to Cleveland's *History of Yates County* (I, 59-60, three trustees of the society tried this method but were victimized by an unscrupulous lawyer and were unsuccessful.

Chapter VII

1. It was the practice of the Phelps-Gorham associates to require the purchaser of a picked township to draw for another township at the same price. Hathaway and Robinson drew the township that was later the site of Geneseo, but gave it up when the Universal Friend objected to her people "trading and buying property at a distance." It was purchased by the Wadsworth family, and turned out to be one of the choicest spots in the Genesee country.

2. Robinson and Hathaway had difficulty in raising the money to pay for their purchase. First they reconveyed a tract of land in the southern part of the township to Oliver Phelps. Then both men transferred their interest in the township to William Carter, Robinson in June, 1793, and Hathaway in August, 1795, about three weeks before his death. Robinson's sale to Carter followed his marriage by about nine months and may have resulted from a breach with the Universal Friend. William Carter was a lawyer from Albany who was interested in land speculation. He visited the Friend's Settle-

ment sometime before February, 1791, and subsequently identified himself as a member of the Universal Friend's society. In purchasing the interest of Robinson and Hathaway in Township Seven of the second range, Carter agreed to confirm the deeds given by these men and to honor receipts for money paid to them. He confirmed the title to the land deeded by Robinson and Hathaway for the use of the Universal Friend to Rachel Malin as trustee in July and August, 1795. But Carter also had difficulty in raising money and was forced to relinquish 4,000 acres in the western part of the township to Oliver Phelps. His letters to Rachel Malin and Oliver Phelps indicate that he never made a satisfactory settlement of his investment in the township. Carter eventually joined the Shaker community at Watervliet and lived there until his death on March 8, 1826 in his eighty-fifth year.

3. Jemima Wilkinson always ate in her own room, sometimes alone and sometimes with Rachel Malin or a special guest. She had her own pewter dishes and table service marked with the initials U. F. No one else used her dishes or utensils. She never ate pork.

Chapter VIII

1. Judge William Potter lived at the Gore for several years, although his wife never left Rhode Island. After his wife's death he sold his property there, and came to New York to live in the home of his son, Arnold, until his death in 1814 at the age of ninety-two. According to a granddaughter he became reconciled with the Universal Friend in his old age, visited her, and even spoke kindly about her. Arnold Potter's wife, Sarah Brown Potter, remained loyal to the Universal Friend.

2. According to some miscellaneous notes made after the death of Jemima Wilkinson but preserved with her papers, Benedict Robinson, as punishment for his marriage, was sentenced to wear a black Quaker cap with folds draped over each shoulder, a type worn by brides, and wore the cap for two or three weeks. This punishment is mentioned in Hudson's biography (p. 169), without identifying the individual. If the incident is true, Robinson's defection could be explained by the resentment he might have felt.

3. John Melish, in *Travels through the United States of America*

(Belfast, 1818), reported on land values in the vicinity of Canandaigua in his entry of November 3, 1811: land which sold twenty years before at a dollar an acre might bring as much as fifty dollars an acre in some places; the average price of uncleared land was from four to six dollars an acre, and of partly cleared land, from eight to twenty-five dollars an acre.

4. The case of Malin *v.* Malin was reported in Wendell, *Reports of Cases,* I, 625. The decision in favor of Rachel and Margaret Malin was by a vote of fifteen to eight in the Court of Errors. Justice Sutherland wrote the decision, which was concurred in by Chief Justice Savage. Senator William M. Oliver of Penn Yan, the person most familiar with the principals of the case, also voted with the majority and wrote a concurring report.

5. Some unpublished attempts to write a refutation to Hudson's book were preserved with the papers of the Universal Friend. Will Turpin advised in a letter in 1822, "I have through life trusted to my own uniform conduct to do away any falsehood that might be uttered against me which I have always found to have done away false impressions on the minds of all that know me, better than for me to have entered into a detailed defense. . . . There is none of us that can expect to pass through life if in any have done any worthy act to raise us above the common, but must be shot at by the mouths of the wicked." His advice prevailed.

Chapter IX

1. This house still stands about four miles north of Branchport, New York. After having a variety of owners it stood empty for several years and fell into disrepair. It was purchased several years ago by Mr. and Mrs. Joseph E. Florance, the present owners, who have carefully restored it.

2. After the death of Rachel Malin in 1847, the portrait came into the possession of James Brown, Jr., and ultimately became the property of his younger daughter, Elizabeth Friend Potter. Mrs. Potter regarded the portrait with an almost superstitious reverence. Although it had hung in the Friend's room while she was alive and was shown freely to visitors to the house after her death, Mrs. Potter

became convinced it was in danger of being stolen or copied, and had it removed from its frame and hidden away in an upstairs cupboard. The explanation for this behavior was a new bit of folklore which seems to have been told first by Mrs. Potter. According to her, the portrait was such a poor likeness that the Friend disliked it and wanted it burned at her death. James Brown asked if he could keep it, so the story went, promising that he would see that it was never copied. Mrs. Potter felt strongly that the portrait should never be exhibited; and if there was no one in the family to inherit it, it should be destroyed. A story exists that Elizabeth Friend Potter got some satisfaction in talking over her problems with the portrait and even propped it up on a chair across the tea table, to "have tea with the Friend." Her son, Arnold Potter, inherited the portrait and set up a public trust in his will to care for the portrait after his death. A decision of the Surrogate designated the Village of Penn Yan as the owner of the portrait, which was to be in the custody of the Yates County Historical Society. The portrait was badly damaged while in the possession of Arnold Potter, but the Village Board authorized its restoration, and it now hangs in the Oliver House on Main Street, the museum of the Yates County Historical Society. By special permission of the Penn Yan Village Board of Trustees, the first photograph of the portrait ever to be published is included in this book. For a more complete story of the portrait see "Portrait of a Prophetess," in *New York History*, October, 1957.

3. For a century and a half the Friend's Burying Ground in Jerusalem was kept inviolate. It was located on the James Brown property, owned in recent times by his grandson, Arnold Potter, to whom it was a sacred spot. When a lumberman tried to convince him during World War II that he should sell the century-old oaks in the cemetery to help in the war effort, he indignantly refused and branded the idea a sacrilege. In his will Arnold Potter left the James Brown farm, including the cemetery, to a young man whom he had befriended. Within six years of Arnold Potter's death, the tall trees that formed a leafy cathedral over the old burying ground were cut and logged out. The unmarked graves that are the last resting place of the followers of Jemima Wilkinson, the earliest pioneers of

Jerusalem Township, now lie under a tangle of weeds, brush, and broken branches.

Chapter X

1. The folk tales repeated here are those that are most familiar or that seem to have some rational explanation. So much nonsense has appeared in print about Jemima Wilkinson that an attempt to correct all the popular errors would be an impossible task. For example, the W. P. A. Guide, *Connecticut* (1938); B. A. Botkin, *A Treasury of New England Folklore* (1947); and I. H. Sperry and W. H. Garrigus, *They Found a Way, Connecticut's Restless People* (1938), all associate Jemima Wilkinson with Ledyard, Connecticut. The details about her career in the last of the three books are so completely different from any other sources of information that they could only have originated in the authors' imaginations. But the Ledyard association must have some explanation, although none has come to light. Ledyard did not even exist as such until it was incorporated in 1836, seventeen years after Jemima's death. It was the North Parish of Groton when Jemima was preaching in the area, and it is likely that she traveled through it on some of her journeys from South Kingstown, Rhode Island. Her Groton followers came from the southern part of the town, however, and it is as doubtful that she even held a meeting in the present town of Ledyard as it is certain that she was not born nor had her vision there.

The term "Jemimakins" is sometimes used in modern accounts to describe the followers of Jemima Wilkinson. The earliest printed incident of the expression discovered in the research for this book was in 1869. It is a derisive epithet that evidently was not used during Jemima's own lifetime and would have been highly offensive to her and her followers, who never recognized her given name but referred to themselves as the Universal Friends.

The name Jemima Wilkinson is an established part of the folklore of a neighborhood that she never visited and probably never heard of. A distinctive group of people known as Pang Yangers lived for several generations in isolation in a section of Lloyd Township in Ulster County, New York. They were supposed to be the descend-

ants of six or seven families of followers of Jemima Wilkinson who
were on their way from Connecticut to join her colony near Penn
Yan, but, instead, settled in this Hudson Valley location. The historical foundation for this folk tale would be an interesting subject
for investigation. None of the material uncovered in the research for
this biography offers an explanation. Harold Harris in "Pang Yang's
Poet-Chronicler" (Warren Sherwood), *New York Folklore Quarterly*, XV (1959), 116-126, introduces the legend.

2. Wilkins Updike, *A History of the Episcopal Church in Narragansett, Rhode-Island* (New York, 1847), p. 285.

Bibliographical Essay

MUCH of the material about Jemima Wilkinson that has appeared in print is entirely worthless to the scholar seeking to make an accurate, dispassionate evaluation of her historical significance. Hardly a decade has passed since her death without the appearance in newspapers and magazines of new articles, written to entertain a popular audience by recounting old folk tales and even by creating new ones. The primary source for most of these accounts was David Hudson's *History of Jemima Wilkinson* (Geneva, N. Y., 1821) and the reprint edition, *Memoir of Jemima Wilkinson* (Bath, N. Y., 1844). Hudson's bias and general inaccuracy was discussed earlier, and his unreliability is confirmed by every student who has made a serious study of her life.

The best article in print is "Jemima Wilkinson" by Robert St. John, in the New York Historical Association's *Proceedings*, XXVIII (1930), 158-175. St. John's bibliography is the most extensive to date, representing a long search for materials for a full-scale biography. When St. John was unable to gain access to the Wilkinson papers in the possession of Arnold Potter, he summarized his factual material in the article and used his information as the basis of a novel, *Jerusalem the Golden* (New York, 1926). Another novel based on the life of Jemima Wilkinson is Carl Carmer's *Genesee Fever* (New York, 1941). Both are good fiction but do not depict the historical Jemima

Wilkinson. Robert St. John's extensive notes were made available to Arnold Potter but disappeared after Arnold Potter's death.

The papers of Jemima Wilkinson and her followers, especially of Margaret and Rachel Malin and James Brown, Jr., were preserved by James Brown, Jr., and were passed on to his daughter, Elizabeth Friend (Mrs. Edson) Potter, and to her son, Arnold Potter. About 1941, Mrs. Walter D. Henricks of Penn Yan persuaded Mr. Potter to use the Wilkinson papers to write an accurate biography of the Universal Friend. Mr. Potter completed a biography, but the manuscript has since disappeared in the confusion following Arnold Potter's death. A few years before he died, Potter, a graduate of Cornell, deposited a selection of the Wilkinson papers with the Collection of Regional History at Cornell University. These were microfilmed with his permission and were to remain at Cornell unless claimed by his heirs after his death. Soon after Arnold Potter's death in 1953, a niece, Mary Leah Potter, claimed the papers at Cornell and took them to her home in Heneker, New Hampshire. Arnold Potter's will provided for a trust to preserve the papers and several other items associated with the Universal Friend. The will was contested by Mary Leah Potter, and a compromise solution was worked out by Surrogate Judge Maurice W. McCann. Mary Leah Potter was ordered to turn over the articles and papers that had belonged to Arnold Potter to the Village of Penn Yan, and the Yates County Historical Society was designated as the custodian of such materials on behalf of the village. Miss Potter returned the portrait of the Universal Friend but seems to have kept many of the papers and probably destroyed them before her death. The microfilm of the Wilkinson papers, made by the Collection of Regional History at Cornell University, is of unique value, since the original documents are no longer available. This microfilm and another microfilm of some papers given by Arnold Potter to John Nicolo of Penn Yan, are the most important sources of primary materials about Jemima Wilkinson and her society. The Collection of Regional History of Cornell University has other Jemima Wilkinson material in the papers collected by Sidney Ayres. Three black notebooks containing transcriptions of some of the Wilkinson papers, several pages of Arnold Potter's manuscript, and comments by Mr. Potter are held for the Yates County Historical Society in the vault of the Yates

County Surrogate in Penn Yan. These notebooks were compiled by Mrs. Henricks when she was working with Arnold Potter.

Not many of the general accounts of Jemima Wilkinson that have appeared in various popular and scholarly periodicals have merit. Perhaps the best is an anonymous article in *Lend A Hand* (Boston), X (1893), 29-30, 77, 126-143, probably written by the editor, Edward Everett Hale. Another article of value was written by James A. Rose in *Potter's American Monthly* (Philadelphia), IX (1877), 377-381. Rose evidently belonged to the Rhode Island family of followers of Jemima Wilkinson and had access to family papers no longer available. Three more recent articles are also useful. "The Universal Friend: Jemima Wilkinson" by Mrs. Walter D. Henricks and Arnold Potter, *New York History*, XXIII (1942), 159-165, used some of the Wilkinson papers for the first time. "New Jerusalem and the Public Universal Friend (Jemima Wilkinson)" by Ruth Upson, *New York Folklore Quarterly*, XI (1955), 20-33, represents the only published results of a long study of the subject. "Jemima Wilkinson: Errant Quaker Divine" by Charles Lowell Marlin, *Quaker History*, Autumn, 1963, is a summary of the author's excellent master's essay. A sympathetic article that is frequently cited is "Jemima Wilkinson, the Universal Friend" by the Rev. John Quincy Adams, in the *Journal of American History*, IX (1915), 249-263; this account is based on a few printed sources and has a number of inaccuracies. The article in the *Dictionary of American Biography* also contains errors of fact. A sketch by the author of this book will appear in *Notable American Women, 1607-1950*. An interesting early article that seems to be almost entirely fictitious is "Jemima Wilkinson, the American Prophetess," by a "Colonel Johnson," in the *Eclectic Magazine*, V (1845), 546-558, reprinted from *Tait's Magazine*.

Chapter I

The most important sources of new material about the Wilkinson family in Cumberland, Rhode Island, was found in the manuscript notes of Abigail (Mrs. Nathan) Sprague. Mrs. Sprague did research and collected material for a town history from about 1890 to 1918. Her manuscript notes are owned by her great-great-grandson, Robert V. Simpson, of Abbot Run Valley Road, Cumberland, who not only made the notes available to the author but helped to locate the various sites in Cumberland associated with Jemima Wilkinson. *Memoirs of the Wilkinson Family* by Israel Wilkinson (Jacksonville, Ill., 1869), includes an excellent chapter on Jemima Wilkinson as well as information on her family. *The Biographical Cyclopedia of Representative Men of Rhode Island* (Providence, 1881) contains useful sketches about Jemima Wilkinson and her father and brother. The records of the Town of Cumberland contain references to the Wilkinson family, including the births of the Wilkinson children. The accounts of disciplinary action against Jemima and others of her family may be found in the records of the Smithfield Monthly Meeting of Women and the Smithfield Monthly Meeting of Men of the Society of Friends. These are available on microfilm at the Rhode Island Historical Society, and the originals, in the vault of the Moses Brown School in Providence, may be examined at a cost of $2.50 an hour.

Chapter II

The most important source on the early career of Jemima Wilkinson is *Enthusiastical Errors, Transpired and Detected,* by Abner Brownell (New London, Conn., 1783). The American Antiquarian Society has a copy of the book, but its scarcity and the fact that it does not refer to Jemima Wilkinson by name have caused it to be overlooked. *The Literary Diary of Ezra Stiles,* edited by Franklin B. Dexter (New York, 1901), three volumes, contains several references to Jemima Wilkinson. *Early History of Brown University, Including the Life, Times, and Correspondence of President Manning* by Reuben A. Guild (Providence, 1897) and several manuscript letters of President James Manning in the Archives of Brown University refer to Jemima Wilkinson. "Plagiarism by a Prophetess" by Herbert A. Wisbey, Jr., in *Rhode Island History,* XX (1961), 65-71, discusses the publication of *Some Considerations, Propounded to the Several Sorts and Sects of Professors of This Age* in 1779.

Chapter III

Manuscript material about Jemima Wilkinson at the Rhode Island Historical Society includes: Rhode Island Historical Manuscripts,

Vol. 14, pp. 119, 125, 135, 235, 237, and 321; the Moses Brown Papers, Vol. 3, p. 36; Vol. 14, p. 5; and Misc. Vol. 2, p. 72; the manuscript diary of the Rev. John Pitman, September 22, 1783; a typewritten copy of the diary of Jeffrey Watson, May 22, 1780; and the diary of Daniel Updike, November 15, 1778 (Shepley Papers, Vol. 15, p. 73). The actual manuscript record, "Petitions to the Rhode Island General Assembly," 1778-79-80, Vol. 17, p. 35, in the Rhode Island State Archives, contains information about the proposed trip to England not included in the printed *Records of the Colony of Rhode Island*, edited by John R. Bartlett (Providence, 1862) VIII, 468-469. The records of the Town of South Kingston contain information about Judge William Potter and James Parker. A typewritten manuscript in the Kingston Public Library, "Kingston Annals, Reminiscences of Little Rest," by the Rev. J. Hagadorn Wells (1817-1907), written in 1897, has some interesting information. The Little Rest Museum in Kingston has a copy of a typewritten paper about the Arthur N. Peckham farm (the site of Judge William Potter's home), written by John G. Erhardt, Jr., in 1949. A useful article is "Little Rest" by Philip Kittredge Taylor, in the *New England Magazine*, XXVIII (1903). A valuable source is *A History of the Episcopal Church in Narragansett, Rhode-Island* by Wilkins Updike (New York, 1847). Useful information may be found in the *East Greenwich News*, June 28, 1928; *History of the Town of East Greenwich* by D. H. Greene (Providence, 1877); *The History of East Greenwich, Rhode Island* by Martha R. McPartland (East Greenwich, 1960); and *Westerly and Its Witnesses* by Frederic Denison (Providence, 1878).

Chapter IV

A Narrative of Thomas Hathaway and His Family . . . by Mrs. William Hathaway, Jr. (New Bedford, Mass., 1869), has considerable material about Jemima Wilkinson but must be used with care. The Land Records, Vol. 23, p. 75, of the Town of New London, Connecticut, lists the ten children of Benjamin Brown, "formerly of Fisher's Island, but late of New London," five of whom were followers of Jemima Wilkinson. Charles R. Stark *Groton, Conn., 1705-1905* (Stonington, Conn., 1922), pp. 138, 165, contains some brief references. The interesting deed to land donated for the Universal

Friends Meeting House in New Milford, Connecticut, is recorded
in Book 16, pp. 22 and 23, of the Land Evidence of the Town of New
Milford. Samuel Orcott's *History of the Towns of New Milford and
Bridgewater, Connecticut, 1703-1882* (Hartford, 1882,), pp. 324-327,
is important. A typewritten manuscript, "Some Significant Events in
the Early History of St. Andrew's Parish," compiled by the Rev.
Willoughby Newton, traces the history of the Universal Friends'
meetinghouse in New Milford. *Doctor Henry Skilton and His De-
scendents* by John Davis Skilton (New Haven, 1921), p. 23, gives
information on the background of Sarah Richards.

Chapter V

The manuscript diary of Christopher Marshall at the Historical
Society of Pennsylvania in Philadelphia is of great value. Marshall,
his sons, and daughter entertained Jemima Wilkinson and her followers whenever they came to Philadelphia, and the arrivals and de-
partures are recorded in his detailed diary. The volume for the year
1782 is a handwritten copy of the original and is not complete. The
original diaries for the years 1783-1785 and 1787-1790 were checked.
The manuscript diary of Elizabeth Drinker, also at the Historical
Society of Pennsylvania, contains references in the entries for October 12, 1782, and August 15, 1784. Other descriptions or references
are located in *Extracts from the Diary of Jacob Hiltzheimer, of
Philadelphia,* edited by Jacob Cox Parsons (Philadelphia, 1893); an
account by "Lang Syne" in *Poulson's American Daily Advertiser,*
July 24, 1828; the "Lang Syne" account in John F. Watson, *Annals
of Philadelphia and Pennsylvania* (Philadelphia, 1905), I, 553-555;
*Our Revolutionary Forefathers, the Letters of François, Marquis de
Barbé-Marbois,* translated by Eugene P. Chase (New York, 1929),
pp. 162-166; *Travels in North America,* by François Jean de Chastellux (London, 1787), I, 288-289; *The American Museum* (Philadelphia), I (1787), 150-154, 218-222, 277-302, 389-392; *The Freeman's
Journal* (Philadelphia), February 14, March 28, August 22, August
29, and September 5, 1787; *Philadelphia Gazette,* March 28 and April
4, 1787; *New Haven Gazette and Connecticut Magazine,* II (1787),
34-36, 57-59.

The *Genealogical Record of the Schwenkfelder Families,* by

Samuel K. Brecht (Pennsburg, Pa., 1923), pp. 1440-1452, contains much valuable material about the Wagener family and Jemima Wilkinson. Other information about Jemima Wilkinson in Worcester is found in several scrapbooks of newspaper clippings in the possession of the Historical Society of Montgomery County in Norristown, Pennsylvania, and in a publication of the society, *Historical Sketches*, VI (1929), 156-168, by Howard W. Kriebel.

Chapter VI

The Wilkinson papers microfilmed by the Collection of Regional History, Cornell University, and the notebooks and miscellaneous papers of Arnold Potter are the basis for much of Chapters VI through IX. Of primary importance is the *History and Directory of Yates County*, by Stafford C. Cleveland, Vol. I (Penn Yan, N.Y., 1873); Vol. II was published for the first time when Vol. I was reprinted in 1951. Cleveland was the editor of the Yates County *Chronicle* and printed much of the material he collected for his history in the newspaper throughout 1869. He collected the reminiscences of early pioneers and followers of Jemima Wilkinson and had access to family papers no longer available. His account, although inaccurate in some specific dates and details, is one of the best accounts of Jemima Wilkinson and her society in print. Important also is the *History of the Pioneer Settlement of Phelps and Gorham's Purchase*, by Orasmus Turner (Rochester, 1851).

The Manuscript Section of the New York State Library in Albany has two important sources for the early settlement: New York Colonial Manuscripts, Land Papers, Vol. L, pp. 83, 88, 91, 111, 112, 113; and letters of William Carter, James Parker, Arnold Potter, and Benedict Robinson, in the Phelps and Gorham papers. The Ruth Prichard Spencer papers, owned by Paul S. Barnes, Old County House Road, Penn Yan, N. Y., include a diary of the trip of Jemima Wilkinson from Philadelphia to the Friend's Settlement. "O'Rielly's Western Mementos," Vol. XV, Document 3, a collection of manuscripts owned by the New-York Historical Society, is a personal account of the early settlement of the Genesee country, by Thomas Morris, written about 1844.

Chapter VII

Many travelers in western New York visited or commented on Jemima Wilkinson. These include John Lincklaen, *Travels in the Years 1791 and 1792 in Pennsylvania, New York and Vermont* (New York and London, 1897), pp. 61-63, 76; *Collections of the Massachusetts Historical Society*, I (1806), 285; William Savery, *A Journal . . . of William Savery* (London, 1844), pp. 58-59, 67-70; Duc de la Rochefoucauld-Liancourt, *Travels through the United States of North America . . .* (London, 1799), I, 110-118; Le Comte de Colbert Maulevrier, *Voyage dans L'intérieur des Etats-Unis et au Canada* (Baltimore, 1935), pp. 40-43: John Maude, *Visit to the Falls of Niagara, in 1800* (London, 1826), p. 54; *The Port Folio* (Philadelphia) Series 3, IV (1810), 235-237; *Balance and State Journal* (Albany), March 19, 1811; *The Christian Disciple*, V (1817), 277-279; *Grosvenor Library Bulletin* (Buffalo) IX (1926), 9. An article repeating material from Hudson, appearing in the *Christian Advocate and Journal* (New York), May 22, 1840, brought a reply from a D. B. W. of Auburn, published on July 3, 1840. The manuscript journals of James Emlen (New York State Library) and of David Bacon (Quaker Collection of the Haverford College Library) contain some additional material on Pickering's treaty of 1794 not included in the printed journal of William Savery.

Chapter VIII

The Wilkinson papers on microfilm contain numerous briefs, depositions, and letters from the lawyers involved in the various cases. Printed reports of three of the cases are in William Johnson, *Reports of Cases*, II (New York, 1848), 321-326; XV (Albany, 1853), 293-297; and John L. Wendell, *Reports of Cases* (Albany, 1829), I, 625-695. Biographical sketches of the lawyers for each side include Thomas R. Gold, *Biographical Directory of the American Congress 1774-1961* (Washington, 1961), p. 953; Elisha Williams, *Dictionary of American Biography* (New York, 1936), XX, 257-258; Abraham Van Vechten, *Cyclopaedia of American Biographies*, VII, 434-435, David Hudson, Geneva (N.Y.) *Courier*, January 18, 1860 (obituary). Only scattered references to the blasphemy trial exist. One of these is *Sally Kane Morris's Reminiscences,* privately printed in New York in 1889, written by Mrs. Thomas Morris of Canandaigua.

Chapter IX

A manuscript of recollections of Jemima Wilkinson related by Mrs. Huldah Barnes Davis in 1890 was copied in a notebook by Walter Wolcott, Village of Penn Yan Historian, in 1927 and is at the Yates County Historical Society. *The National Intelligencer* (Washington, D.C.) carried two obituaries, on July 21 and July 28, 1819, and a letter to the editor on September 11, 1819. *The American Republican* (Downington, Pa.) contained some original comments by editor Charles Mowry on July 20 and July 31, 1819. The will of Jemima Wilkinson is recorded in the Ontario County Surrogate's Office in Canandaigua, New York. The division of her lands among the relatives of Rachel and Margaret Malin may be traced in the deeds recorded in the Yates County Clerk's Office in Penn Yan, New York.

Chapter X

Several of the folk tales were collected in interviews in Rhode Island, Connecticut, Pennsylvania, and New York.

Index